North Country Cabin

Edward Flaccus

Illustrated by the author

MOUNTAIN PRESS PUBLISHING COMPANY
MISSOULA, 1979

Published simultaneously in Canada by
SAMUEL–STEVENS, PUBLISHERS
TORONTO

Library of Congress Cataloging in Publication Data

Flaccus, Edward, 1920-
    North country cabin.

    Bibliography: p.
    Includes index.
    1. Log cabins—Design and construction. I. Title.
TH4840.F55   694'.2   78-21638
ISBN 0-87842-111-4   0-88866-601-2 (Canada)

ii

To my family:

Sally, Jennifer, Chris, and Lynne
for all their love, support, and help.

To the many students of Bennington College and
other friends who shared their time and care:

Annelies Allain • Jean-pierre Allain • Clay Andres
Tom Andres • Lynne Chapman • Cindy Chevins
Charles Collins • Blair Cooke • Stephen Davis
Albert Edge • Marie Emlen • Alex Epstein
Kathy Estes • Lou Flaccus • Ruth Flaccus
Tom Gates • Rabbit Goode • Martha Hart • Helms
Don Hochstrasser • Doug Houston • Jyl Jones
Cindy Kallet • Kathy Kingston • Carol Kino
Lloyds • Beth Mckay • Melissa Marshall
Jim Martin • Betsy Meyer • Art Myers
David Myers • Ellie Myers • Emlen Myers
Will Myers • Don Raina • Mike Raina
John Raskin • Michele Reardon • Sally Sandberg
Tia Stack • Fred Steele • Ted Steele
George Vos • Alice Wimer • George Woodwell.

And to Skye

who has since gone to the sunny fields where
there are bitches of great beauty and bones
without end.

Contents

vi

_f

First Words

Out of the need for more living space, a supply of red pines that are both big enough and need thinning, and not least from a long-felt desire to build a log cabin, comes this enterprise. From hard work shared with many friends, the cabin grows into its place in the woods, as if it had always meant to be there, favored by the landscape and gently favoring it in return.

This cabin rises in the woods of north-central New Hampshire, but it could as well take shape anywhere in the North Country, from Maine to Minnesota or in the vast expanse of Canada, from the Maritimes westward through Quebec and Ontario and beyond to the North and West. In that great North Country there is much shared: fragrant conifers and glacial lakes, lovely rivers,

1

wildflowers and northern birds, moose and deer and foxes, laughing loons and yes, even mosquitoes and deer flies and black flies.

Conifer-log cabins can do as well in the Rockies, whether in the northern mountains or further south where the subalpine and montane conditions prevail at higher elevations. Here, and even in the Pacific Coast Conifer Forest Region, there are suitable logs and lovely country, clear streams with their enthusiastic trout, and wildflowers, birds, and other animals to nourish the spirit.

What follows is not just a "how to do it" book, though it might serve somewhat in that fashion. Rather, it is a chronicle of how a particular cabin comes to be built, on weekends and vacations over a period of two years, not merely as a construction job, but as a moonlighting piece of life including family, students, and non-student friends, and dogs and a cat, and last but hardly least, nature in all its variety and beauty.

There will be enough detail and drawings in the telling to help others cope with some such project, but hopefully there will be enough beyond to serve as some kind of celebration.

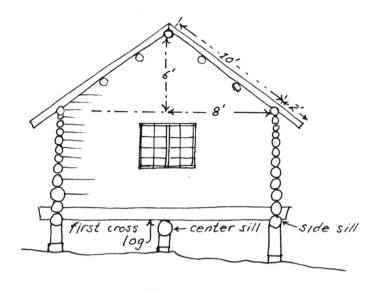

first cross log | ← center sill | ← side sill

From Intention to Plan

If you build something, you ought to have a plan. In the old days I suppose early cabin builders developed such in their heads, kept them there, and followed the mental picture in the building. That was in a time when more people had more of the skills, having learned them from experience — working with an old-time expert, perhaps. What looked right and what didn't, what worked and what didn't had been worked out by hundreds of years of trials and errors, and there would always be someone handy to help with either directions or advice.

Such ready access to experience in the shape of old-time jacks and masters of many trades is not so often available now. What we have is books, and I manage to get hold of four older ones that are wholly or at least in part devoted to how to build a log cabin. While none is great by itself, they all have good and useful information in them, and looking them over adds greatly to my recollections of cabins I've seen. I am to benefit more later by closer attention to specific sections in one or the other, when I come to the floor, the walls, the roof, etc. For now they give a general picture of what is possible, and the next step is to sit down with pencil and paper and make a series of rough sketches.[1]

Through several cool weekend evenings of late summer I sit by the fire with pencil and paper, thinking through the what and the how, trying proportions. The family reads; the dogs and Mucho the cat lie contentedly dreaming of past and future pleasures.

The dogs are Shelties; Skye, aging tricolor native of Minnesota has been joined by new young sable females being raised by Sally and Lynne. A succession of them will come and go during the cabin raising: Kippen Dairsey Maid of Kintyre, Lochy, Clixby and Claxby, Peebles, Weebelo and

---

[1] In the last year or two, several excellent how-to-do-it books have been published; see Appendix.

4

Tarn, Shuna, Twiggles, and Jesse. Lochy is the ranking bitch, trained to obedience championship by Lynne and winner of numerous trophies. It is Sally who spins the roulette wheel of canine genes, contriving marriages like some queen planning royal succession, poring over pedigrees and choosing studs from Maine to Massachusetts. She is concentrating on temperament and chooses well, for the puppies are bright, handsome, stable and affectionate. Shelties are Shetland Sheep Dogs, and are an interesting breed. Small and rather delicate looking, they are actually quite tough, fast, and very intelligent. Their heritage is one of a working dog for herding sheep, though most of the working sheep dogs nowadays in Britain are Border Collies. Some characteristic Sheltie habits are endearing: a stylized sneeze that demonstrates pleasure, and a propensity for sleeping on their backs with feet in air.

Lochy is a veteran of many shows, including four in St. Johns, New Brunswick, where she dis-

Lochy

Mucho

Peebles

tinguishes herself with three firsts, a highest scoring dog in trial, and her Canadian C.D.

But back to the cabin. I know I want to build a "classic" northern log cabin, low, simple, but rather large. I've decided on the saddle notch for the corners. In the strip stand of red pine down by the road I have a practically inexhaustible source of logs to 12 inches at the butt and up to 40 or so feet long.

Red pine is what's available, so that's what we will use. Actually you can use almost any species. In the Southern Appalachians cabins run to hardwoods, often hewn square and even dovetailed at the corners. But northern cabins are made from softwoods (conifers), most all of which grow tall and straight if in a well-stocked stand, and a suitable choice can be made from white or red or even jack pine, red or white or black spruce, or northern white cedar or tamarack. If I had a choice I'd prefer white pine, which has a wonderful light strength and cuts clean; or white cedar, light and fragrant and decay resistant; or red spruce, heavier and harder but clean-cutting. But the other spruces and red and jack pine are perfectly satisfactory. You can even make do with balsam fir, soft and decay-prone though it is. What one wants is tall trees, relatively limbless and with minimum taper. To the extent that prudence overcomes Bunyanesque bravado, you'll keep butt diameters under 14 or so inches, at least if much solo building is

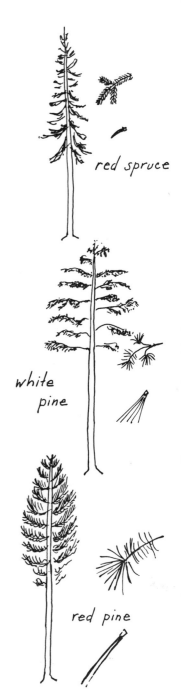

red spruce

white pine

red pine

7

involved. For more detailed information on the characteristics of the different tree species, see Appendix.

For Westerners there is an abundance of suitable trees: lodgepole pine, at higher elevations and ponderosa pine at lower, Western white pine in Idaho, larches and cedars and hemlocks, Engelmann Spruce and subalpine fir (and other spruces and firs), and of course the Doug fir that isn't a fir at all. I'm familiar with most but haven't actually worked with many of them. Judging from appearance, I'd rate lodgepole and larch right at the top for relative limblessness and lack of taper, but any of them growing in well-stocked youngish stands would make fine cabin logs.

I sketch out a design, 24 feet long by 16 feet wide, with 2 windows and the front door on the south side, 2 windows on the north, a double window on the east or kitchen end (for morning sun), and a window, door, and small upstairs window at the west or loft end. A 3 in 8 pitch to the roof will give 6 feet headroom in the center of the loft. A happy spin-off from this choice is that each half elevation of the roof is a 3-4-5 triangle, making for easy figuring.

An early decision rules out a fireplace. Fireplaces are very comforting, in spring and fall and during cold summer northeasters. But during northern winters they are terrible heat-losers, net producers of cold rather than warmth, and ravenous consumers of wood. A North Woods

8

cabin shouldn't have one. I plan instead for a stove, a farm kitchen wood range. Such are not as efficient as the modern air-tight stoves, but they provide the cooking function, even to an oven.

I now draw careful scale elevations of each of the four sides on graph paper, sizing and locating the windows and doors for good proportion, and for the 2'x3' barn sash windows I know are available and cheap. I figure on a center sill to support the floor joists in the middle, and three purlins on each side in the roof, between the ridge and the plates (these are later reduced to two purlins per side). Very soon I modify the plan to include a porch at the loft end, by extending the roof out that end by 10 feet.

And so outdoor work begins.

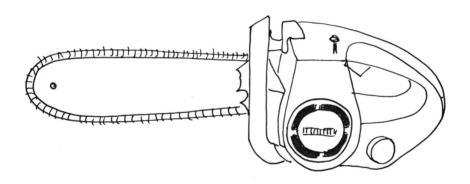

Cutting the Logs
and Siting

I know that I will need about 20 long logs about 35 feet long, and about 20 cross logs about 25 feet long, so I cut down about 50 trees the first fall, limbing them. The plan is to have them hauled up to the site and piled there in late fall (it turns out my friend Ned with the tractor doesn't get to it till spring). I mark the trees in a regular thinning operation and cut them down and limb them with a 14" bar lightweight chainsaw. This saw is to prove a great boon through the whole construction process, and will be the only power tool used. I block as many of the logs as I can off the ground, and they go to their winter bed, soon covered by snow.

Siting is an important operation, and we do it while I am cutting the logs. A couple of hundred yards away, just far enough into the second growth conifer-hardwoods behind the house to be hidden, I find a suitable spot. The ground slopes somewhat to the North; I would have preferred a slope to the South, but none is available in the immediate area. A rather dense stand of hemlock provides protection on the North and West, and some earlier selective logging to the South and West has opened up an area that allows winter sunshine. Thus are met the basic North Woods requirements of protection from the cold winter winds and provision for sun from the South.

On several crisp fall days, after the leaves are down, Jenny and Lynne help clear the site. As we start very early one morning we hear geese calling; in a large and fluid V high overhead, they are Canadas headed south, to the bays south of the Cape, to the Sound, or Chesapeake. The excitement in their voices is contagious. With a larger

11

FELLING

1. undercut (saw)

2. chop out notch

3. saw in above notch

4. drive in wedge

chain saw we fell a big hemlock, a couple of large red maples, a spruce or two, and assorted smaller trees. Jenny is getting the hang of the chain saw, and is delighted by the shower of clean white sawdust that decorates her dark Norwegian sweater. A tall and beautiful girl, she has inherited from her grandmother Flaccus that intimacy of relating to nature with her emotions and all her senses. A big and a smaller spruce — both tall and straight — will be joined later by a couple of other spruce nearby and will later find their way into the walls of the cabin. Several huge piles of slash accumulate — hemlocks are especially well-endowed with branches — which we burn after the first snowfall. The red maple and hemlock logs are to be used to support the peeled cabin logs off the ground to dry. After that duty the maple at least will be worked into firewood for the cabin stove. A roadway is swamped out the fifty yards or so into the woods from the field to the site. Presiding not far from what will be the southeast corner of the cabin is a huge white pine; there are two others nearby, all tall, straight and limbless, testifying that around the turn of the century they began in a small forest clearing or at least grew together with other trees in a dense stand.

With the plans drawn, the trees cut, and the site cleared we wait out the winter. It's time for a tool inventory. In addition to the small chainsaw, I have assorted axes, an antique carpenter's adze, a drawknife, braces and bits, a peavy and a cant hook (essentially a short handled peavy without a point at the end), a sledge hammer, a variety of chisels, plus the usual range of carpenter's tools: squares, plumbob, level, planes from block to jack, crosscut and rip handsaws, chalk line and line level, metal tapes and wooden rules. I order a block and tackle, a log chain, some pulp hooks, a two-hooked log carrier, and a picaroon. The log carrier and the picaroon turn out to be white elephants; the former heavy beyond reason. We will scarcely use them, and the pulp hooks will barely earn their keep.

Later, when crews of volunteers will come to peel, we'll need more drawknives. I pick up an old one at a bargain price, Bob lends me one, and Jim lends me a small beauty that becomes a favorite, so there are four.

I get a set of carpenters dividers for notch-marking, and bring up from College a hundred foot tape and a Suunto clinometer.

Far and away the king of cabin-building tools is the axe. If you have a sharp axe and know how to use it, you can do just about anything. I have my

TOOLS I

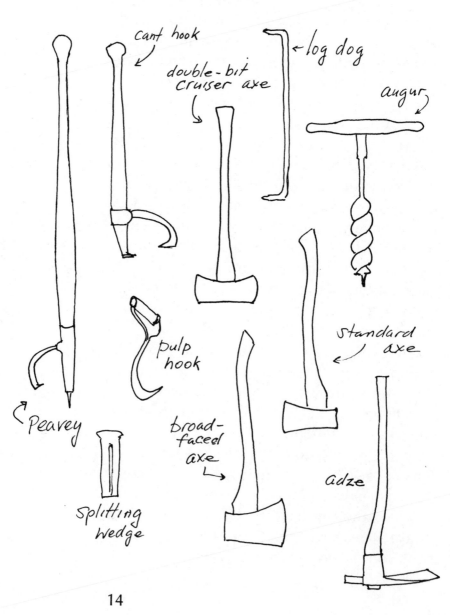

cant hook

double-bit
cruiser axe

←log dog

augur

pulp
hook

standard
axe

Peavey

broad-
faced
axe

splitting
wedge

adze

own double-bitted cruiser axe, wonderfully light, with a 24" ironwood handle polished smooth by use. I keep it razor sharp and it is my special favorite. There are heavier axes for the heavier jobs. With axes we will limb, smooth the limb knots, notch, and do the countless little jobs of shaping, hewing, cutting, etc.

Learning to use an axe takes time, which working with and observing an expert will shorten. And as with any skill, there's no substitute for experience. I learned a lot, many years ago, from New England handyman Stokes (who also taught me how to scythe), a Forest Service Ranger by the name of Corbett, and an Indian in Trenton, North Dakota named Pete Falcon. Pete, a kind of ageless leader in the local community of his tribe, was a fine and gentle and modest man, and a wizard with the axe. But such help aside, axmanship, after all, is not brain surgery, and anyone who is vigorous, prudent, somewhat coordinated and diligent can acquire some skill. Somewhere along the way there may be an accident — mine came when I was a 15-year-old trying to show myself how good I was at standing on a horizontal log and cutting halfway through from each side. The axe glanced off the rain-wet log and hit the bottom of my shin just above the ankle, exposing clean white bone in a crisp 2-inch cut. Not much meat there. I was so ashamed I never told anyone

TOOLS II

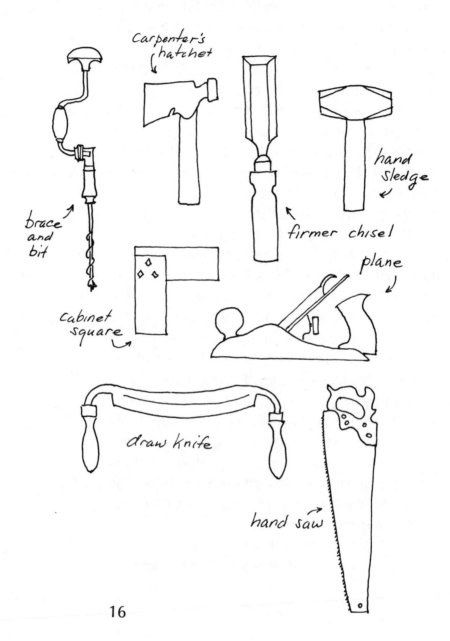

Carpenter's hatchet

hand sledge

firmer chisel

brace and bit

plane

Cabinet square

draw knife

hand saw

and just pulled the cut together with adhesive. The unstitched cut left me branded for life with a pretty broad scar. I've never had another axe accident in the forty-two years since.

Axe sizes and weights vary, and the thing to do is to find what suits you best, and put that together with the nature of the job to be done. Also, how much "cheek" you leave when grinding and sharpening will affect performance in limbing, say, versus chopping through larger logs. That's one advantage of a double-bitted axe: you can sharpen the two sides differently.

There is a truism of considerable applicability from fish to plants to politicians, to the effect that the environment shapes the individual (increasingly since Darwin and Mendel we've known the whys). Though there's no genetic basis for this with axes, it applies. In the Pacific Northwest, for example, the axes are big, heavy, and long-handled; they have to deal with the big trees — Douglas fir, western hemlock, sitka spruce, to say nothing of the coast redwood of northern California.

During those winter evenings of planning, my mind wanders along byways of North Woods experience. There were the ten years we lived in Duluth, a city built on lumber fortunes before it ever turned to mining. Moose and bear not un-

known in the streets even in our day. To the North the wild expanse of the Boundary Waters Canoe country, in which, when I wasn't teaching at the University of Minnesota, Duluth, I did forest ecology research, and on weekends camped and canoed and fished for speckled trout, rainbows and browns, and for the great steelhead that came up the rivers out of Lake Superior to spawn in the spring. It was Holly who taught me the arcane art of steelhead fishing.

Whenever we could make the trip, almost every summer, we would drive East to New Hampshire. To avoid the traffic to the south we'd head due East to the Sault, through Iron River and Ashland, Wisconsin, then through Ironwood and Wakefield, Marquette and Munising and Newberry in upper Michigan to Sault St. Marie. With three young kids we'd load the station wagon and drive straight through without stopping at a motel, all the way to

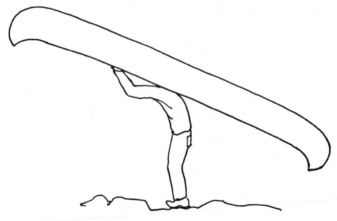

New Hampshire, 36 hours or so, trading off driving and stretching out in the back for some sleep. We were younger then! Wild country in that first stretch, with interesting sugar maple-yellow birch-hemlock on the ridges alternating with long wild low stretches of spruce and fir and northern white cedar interspersed with muskeg.

From the Sault we'd drive east on the Trans-Canada Highway, route 17, with the country getting wilder. Canadian Shield country – old rocks, with jack pine and some white and red pines on rock ridges and sandy outwash, hardwood-conifer mixtures on the till soils, and black spruce, fir, tamarack, white spruce and cedar in the lowlands. Thessalon, Blind River, Massey and Espanola, past the North Channel of Lake Huron and on to the moonscape of Sudbury and Coniston, where extracting three-fourths of the world's nickel has exacted a price. Here sulfur dioxide from the smelting had killed off all the vegetation as much as 20 miles downwind. It was a somewhat depressing ecological lesson (an eternal optimist, I'm hopeful that by now better pollution abatement measures have been taken than building taller stacks). But we always stopped in a good little Chinese restaurant in Sudbury, which cheered us some.

Then on to Sturgeon Falls and North Bay on the north of Lake Nippissing, and down the Ottawa

River through Mattawa, Deux Rivieres, Deep River and Pembroke (Algonquin Park to the South we never got to). This was really the most beautiful part of the trip, with views across the big River into the great Frontier Country of Quebec, essentially roadless, most of the way from Mattawa to Ottawa. I was told the Ottawa River was the route of the early fur traders on the way to Georgian Bay and on west. That provided an historical link to Duluth and Grand Portage northeast of Grand Marais.

From just west of Ottawa, Route 17 threads the St. Lawrence Lowlands, farmlands and towns, all the way to Montreal. Depending on when we left, we'd often see the green roofs of the Houses of Parliament at Ottawa on the second morning and get lost in Montreal several hours later. Or, we'd hit Montreal in the wee hours of the morning; it was at the last dawn, then, when the desire to sleep became overwhelming.

What a huge and beautiful country it was, North Woods all the way from Duluth to Ottawa. And then on the last leg after the lowlands, North Woods again through the Green Mountains of Vermont to the White Mountains of New Hampshire. Pines and spruces, firs and cedar and tamarack, glacial lakes and granitic bedrock, outwash sands and muskegs, and conifer-hardwood forests on the better soils. Wild country then – I hope still. Country with cold winters and snow that stays, where snowshoes and more recently cross country skis earn their keep.

Log cabin country.

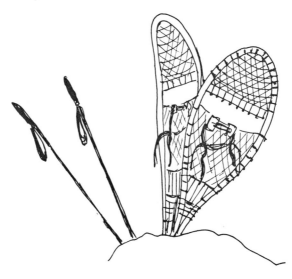

Peeling

Spring comes, and with it the phoebes that always build on top of the light over the front door, and the tree swallows that vie with the bluebirds for the boxes. Work keeps me at College, so I miss the shining white bloom of hobble bush and shad and high bush cranberry, and the white and yellow and blue violets, and the trilliums. But early summer finally comes and with it vacation, welcome respite from the 60 hour weeks of term time. All the logs pulled up by the

22

cat are in one big pile exactly where the cabin is to go. Chris, out of school earlier than I, is already at the peeling, which must be done by laborious drawknifing. He has been hampered by frequent rain showers, but even so has already done a number of logs by the time I come.

The best time to cut most species for easy peeling is during the first couple of weeks of spring growth, at which time the sap is full in the trees and the bark more easily separated. Botanists know that in this brief period the vascular cambium has begun its auxin inspired rapid growth, and the proliferation of new young cells creates a soft tissue between bark and wood, making separation easier. Failing that easiest time, if the logs are peeled immediately after felling during the

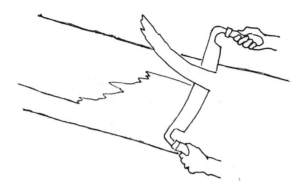

mid-summer, things go easier. Some species, for example white spruce (red spruce is the native species hereabouts), give up their bark with grace; in the early summer pulp cutters can score the bark and pry it off in sheets with a spud bar or axe. I don't know whether you can do that with red spruce, but I do know that red spruce that has been dead more than a year hangs on to its bark with a desparate, vice-like death grip. Other species, red pine and white pine among them, can't really be peeled in sheets at all, at least not until they are bigger and older. Due to the exigencies of our time schedule, we can't work on our red pine logs till the early summer following their fall cutting, and thus the laborious draw-knifing. As each log is peeled, we roll it upslope onto the hemlock and maple ramp logs, to dry as much as possible.

24

In our peeling we remove some but not all of the shining white and juicy underbark, composed of cambium plus phloem; at this stage it matches the white sapwood, which botanists know as xylem. Later we'll discover that the underbark turns dark brown as it dries, darkening the logs; but much later still, as the wood itself shrinks, the dried brown strips can be flaked off.

As bad luck would have it, it has been a rainy spring and early summer; this plus the opportunity that a few months with bark on has provided several species of beetles, results in considerable beetle activity plus blue-stain fungus stains. It is the beetles which spread the fungus, the latter a species of the genus *Ceratocystis* that quickly attacks pine logs if they are left lying in the woods and stains the wood a bluish color, thus reducing the value of the wood as lumber. So our logs are discolored some, though not weakened structurally. Interestingly, the discoloration occurs in radial bands, which indicates the fungus must spread most readily along the vascular rays.

The beetles are of two types: one a long-chested little bark beetle that lays eggs just under the bark. The grubs of this one gallery just under the bark, tracing attractive patterns; these are the grubs that get sliced up by the drawknives as we do our work, and they seem to be the main interest of the winter wren we see browsing along

the logs. The other type of beetle has grubs which, being more adventuresome, eat their way deeper into the wood. It is these latter that the ichneumons seem to be after. There are several species of ichneumons which lay their eggs deep in the wood of trees on or near borer beetle grubs. These parasitic wasps have long, horsehair-like ovipositors which they deploy in a loop and force into the wood at just the right spot to reach a grub or grub tunnel, and through which an egg is laid that will hatch into a larva that will feed on the grub. As a child I remember watching amazed as some — a different and bigger species I think — worked up and down the trunks of the huge living sugar maples in front of our neighbor Minnie Clark's house. Now there are many days during which the backtiring toil of log peeling is lightened by watching several ms. ichneumons running along the logs, only to stop, set up their drill rigs and drill away. How do they know where to drill? Since they continually flick their antennae along the surface of the log, we decide they must get some faint vibration signal through these, from the chewing grub.

Once the logs are peeled, they are no longer of interest to these species of borer beetles or bark beetles. That is a reason why you should certainly peel your logs; other reasons are that peeled logs are neater and cleaner and easier to treat with preservative. On more than one occasion in my life I've slept in cabins of unpeeled spruce to the often loud refrain of the gnawing of grubs deep in the logs.

By late June the trilliums are in fruit,both the painted trillium *(Trillium undulatum)* and the one that goes by the name of "wet dog trillium" or "stinking benjamin" *(Trillium erectum)*. The latter is appropriately named — it has the unpleasant odor so often associated with dark or dull red flowers that are pollinated by flies. The Canada mayflower is past flower, and clintonia and bunchberry are blooming. A winter wren tinkles its rambling squeaky song nearby, the whitethroat keeps calling Tom Peabody in pure sad notes, and the red squirrels scold with their staccato wooden-clock noises. Cheering us onward are the confident, extended and cheerful whistle of the rose-breasted grosbeak, the manic "whip three cheers" of the olive-sided flycatcher, the sharply insistent and repetitious "teacher teacher teacher" of the ovenbird, and the occasional and more distant burred song of the scarlet tanager. Good companions. We are somewhat less enthusiastic that the black flies, mosquitoes, and deer flies are out in force, their numbers swelled by the rainy weather. This unholy triumvirate comes forth somewhat in that order, but with enough overlap to earn the triumvirate designa-

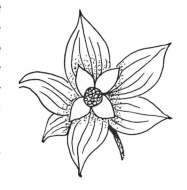

tion. Each has its own character. The black flies can be a scourge; special to the colder spruce-fir North Woods, they hover in clouds around one's head, showing an annoying curiosity about eyes (I wish I had a dollar for every one that has made it into its watery grave in my eyes). All the while the diversionary tactic of eye-buzzing is going on, some are quietly infiltrating behind the lines, into hair, around ears, at the belt line, and up under pant legs. There is often no telltale warning bite — instead the sneaks inject their poison unnoticed, and the itching swollen bite may last for days. I console myself that they are here nowhere near as bad as I've seen them in Penobscot-Katahdin country.

Mosquitoes are geographically more widespread, predictable, and familiar. Slow, deliberate fliers, they give themselves away by their audible whine, and are easily slapped. In moderate numbers, they can be dealt with. It is a different story in the Canadian arctic and in some salt marshes; and I remember canoe portages in Minnesota where hordes of hungry mosquitoes followed along under the canoe, clearly and exultantly recognizing the defenseless condition of their human target.

The bigger deer flies or copperheads — themselves smaller cousins of the horseflies — are predominantly head-buzzers, but their bite,

28

when they get around to it, is sudden and painful. The eternal head-circling is annoying, but as the English did with the V-1 rockets over London, you worry about them when the noise stops. But there are seldom more than two or three of them around you at once, and they're fairly easy to get either by slapping when they land or by catching with cupped hand in mid-air — a skill I mastered as a boy.

No catalogue of insect trials is complete without no-see-ums (we used to call them minges, and I've heard them referred to as punkies), though they don't bother us during the days of cabin work. They can on occasion be the worst of all, since they are barely visible and come right through screens. I never could understand how such a minute creature, barely visible, could pack such a wallop in its bite; en masse they are like fire on the face. They are worst at night, but fortunately they are bad hereabouts on only some few nights a summer, presumably at times of hatches.

All of these pests "go with the territory" of the North Woods, whether it be in Maine or Nova Scotia, Upper Michigan, northern Wisconsin and Minnesota or Quebec and Ontario. They put the outdoorsmen and women to the test, and the trials can be fearsome. I often wonder how the voyageurs dealt with them, before the days of

612 and Off and Cutter's; was it even before the days of oil of citronella or the lovely-smelling mixtures of citronella and tar that I used as a boy on countless trout-fishing expeditions? I've read somewhere that in Colonial New England they sometimes used rancid bear grease (a case of the cure being worse than the disease?), perhaps a New World version of Tibetan rancid yak grease.

Actually, the woods-wise learn the habits of avoidance: that you are relatively free from north woods (not salt-marsh) mosquitoes and black flies (but not deer flies) in the hot sun, and from all of them in the wind, and that no-see-ums are really only a problem at dusk, evening, and dawn. And that campfire smoke helps, if your eyes can stand it. And that heavy clothing is a kind of armor. And that cursing can provide a limited kind of psychological relief. And that all four pests diminish as the summer slips toward fall.

By now I've pitched up the seat of my forest green pants from sliding along astride the logs working the drawknife; resin oozes out into little bead-like droplets on the surface of the peeled wood. Thus I gain a waterproof seat.

The old tent — an early single-pole model used for years by my father on his trout-fishing expeditions, and on its very last legs — is set up as our tool shed at the edge of the site. Beside it we put the old farm grindstone that will help keep the tools sharp. The stone is useful for sharpening the tools of harder steel like the drawknives, but for axes I prefer mill bastard files, which are quicker.

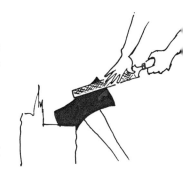

Skye the tricolor Sheltie looks back on ten years of varied experience, from being hit by a car in East Lansing, to three porcupine encounters, to hunts of woodchucks and racoons, to fights too numerous to remember that bespoke more courage than good sense (always with much bigger dogs which always got him down but never could get him to quit). And there were the usual dog affairs of the heart, which included the siring of at least one wildcat litter up the street in Duluth. He has always been specially attached to me, and now he is a constant companion. Whenever I go to work he traipses along behind, to lie in the shade of the big pine, or under the flap of the tool tent, to watch

and to sleep. He will follow through the two years abuilding, lending support by his presence, insinuating it into the very soul of the cabin. When it is raised and roofed he will take to sleeping underneath, where in summer it is shady and cool.

As I write this he is sleeping under the completed cabin. The walk up from the house is now arduous for his arthritic joints and 13-year-old emaciated frame, but he will not miss it. The steadfast fires as they must for dogs and men are burning low, and his days are mostly filled with sleep and dreams, of the glories of yesterdays, of both defeats and triumphs. How I will miss him!

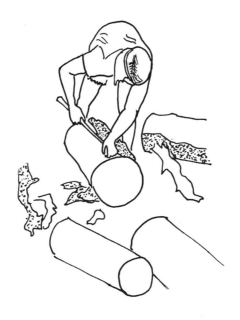

Foundations

Anybody who builds a cabin better support it well off the ground, if he wants it to last a while. The sill logs have to be up off moist mother earth. They could be supported by big rocks, rock or concrete pillars, or even by big cross-cuts of some decay-resistant species of tree like cedar, the way Brooks did his cabin on the North Shore of Lake

33

Superior. On much of the rocky terrain of the Canadian Shield of Ontario, such posts would be a fine choice. My choice is concrete pillars, with a difference. I've seen a cabin or two on tall cylinders of concrete (poured into cardboard cylinders called sonotube) and I didn't like the looks. Tom, a wood-working friend, has suggested wood posts, because they could more easily be braced if necessary. I doubt the bracing will be necessary, but wood will look better. The solution is cylinders down to below frost line in the ground but only up to a little above ground-level, upon which will rest wood posts which in turn support the sills. As luck will have it there is a wolf tamarack in the midst of a youngish white pine stand down toward the road. Tamarack is hard and strong and decay resistant, so we cut the tree to be used for posts, and Don, Chris and I peel the logs immediately. The bark comes off easily in great sheets.

I've decided on pillars 6 feet apart along each

34

of the three sills — a total of 12 under the cabin proper and 3 more under the porch. That means 15 holes to be dug, and we dig them about 2½ feet deep; safe enough I figure in spite of what you hear about frost depth. Maximum penetration of frost takes place in the open, but even then under the insulation of a blanket of snow it would seldom if ever get to three feet in central New Hampshire. Usually, in the woods in an early snow year (early, before the cold weather) the frost doesn't get down — in fact the soil doesn't freeze at all. Without the insulation of snow it's a different matter. The deepest penetration of frost I remember was in Duluth, Minnesota; in one very cold winter it went down 7 feet, but only under streets that were kept bare of snow by plowing. Some of the waterpipes, buried 7 feet, froze that year.

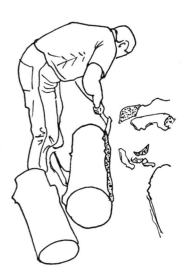

At least one of the planned, spaced holes for a support pillar for the center sill comes right where the stump of a big hemlock is, making digging there impossible. We simply move the hole. We're lucky that doesn't happen with the side sills, for there a move from the planned spacing would show and look wrong.

We stick the sonotube sections into the holes, and getting a ready-mix truck in the narrow drive (quite a trick) close enough to reach a few of the holes with its chute, we pour on August 2, wheel-

ing the concrete along boards to the holes we can't reach with the chute. Fellow-botanist Fred Steele and I split a load — he is pouring a cement cellar floor 2 miles away — and it works out just fine. He brings a clutch of nephews along to help us pour, and Chris and Don and I go over afterward to help with his floor. Sometimes things work out just right; there's just enough concrete to do both jobs. In the top of each pillar we insert an 8'' bolt in the wet concrete; these will fit up into holes in the bases of the tamarack posts.

A ready-mix truck seems almost too much of a sell-out to inappropriate technology, but it saves a lot of time. It may well be out of the question where you decide to build, in which case you'll need to borrow a little gas-engine mixer or else fall back on hand mixing the concrete in a sheet-metal tray. That prospect might persuade you to use rocks or log cross-cuts as piers.

The next day Chris and I peel the cardboard off the 15 pillars (you'd better *not* wait on this till after it dries). We set stakes along all three lines of pillars and with a clinometer used as a sighting level, run chalk lines tight at the appropriate level for sill bottoms. Appropriate level in this case means high enough on the uphill side so that the sill in place will be at least a good foot off the ground, to remain high and dry. All we have to do then is measure down from the chalk line to the

36

top of the concrete for the length of each tamarack post, which we then custom cut from the peeled tamarack logs.

In one of our few concessions to the boon of electricity, we take the posts to the barn and drill ⅝″ holes into the bottom ends with an electric drill. Even so, drilling holes in endgrain tamarack is no easy job.

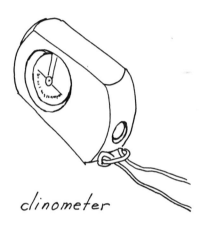

clinometer

SILL SUPPORT

1. concrete pillars are poured in sonotube, each to ~ 6" above ground. 5/8" bolt embedded in top of each, while concrete is wet

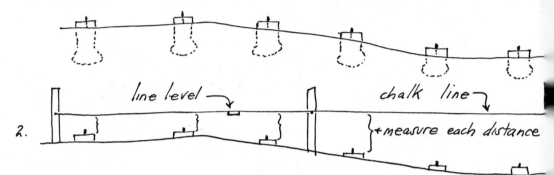

2.

line level →   chalk line ↘

+measure each distance

when concrete is set, peel off sonotube, allow pillars to dry. drive stakes in at each end and in middle. decide on appropriate height to bottom of sill, and drive nail into stake at upper end. attach chalk line and stretch __tight__. using line level or clinometer drive nail at correct height at other end. now measure down from line to top of each post, add 2" for notch in sill, and record measurements. cut a post for each, drill hole in bottom end to accept bolt, and install posts.

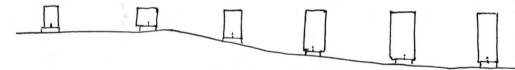

3. measure correct distances along sill and cut 2" deep notches. using tripod at each end and block and tackle, install sill.

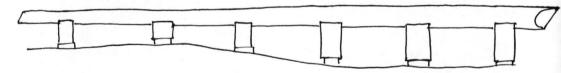

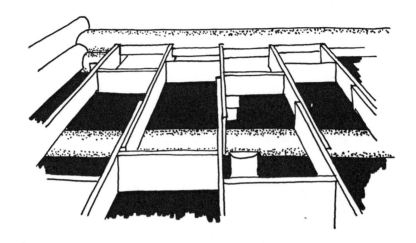

Sills and
Floor

We pick the three biggest, straightest logs for
the sills. The floor joists will rest on 2x4's spiked
onto the insides of the two side sills; hence the
middle sill has to be set in just enough lower so
that the 2x8 joists will rest level on top of it. That
involves some fussing with measurements, but it
is no great problem. Each sill is notched on the
underside to accept the top of its tamarack post.

Setting the sills on top of the posts is the only job requiring use of our block and tackle, suspended from 10 foot high log tripods we'd built; the logs are much too heavy to lift directly up with only back power. Once the sill logs are set we can, using a peavy and/or cant hook, roll all subsequent logs up log ramps into position. Once the two end cross logs are notched in place, we put in the floor joists on 2 foot centers, resting them on

the center sill and on the spiked 2x4's at each end, and spike them in. The joists are 2x8's of New Hampshire spruce, in 10 foot lengths, lapped over the center sill. We saw a 2 foot length off one of each pair, so there is a 2 foot overlap left, and use the extra pieces as spacers between the joists to hold them against twisting. The subfloor will be 1x6 pine roofers, and we lay these down temporarily so we can walk around.

Roofers are tongue-and-groove in varied lengths, and are the only other category of dimension lumber used in the cabin — for subfloor, floor

40

of loft, and for the roof itself. Most roofers you get these days are cheap grade white pine; ours happen to be red pine, which seems appropriate for a red pine log cabin. Red pine is a little harder than white, is no stronger, and doesn't work nearly as well. But for our purposes it is fine.

I let Chris and Doug set the joists, and they do a good job, except that they don't put the spacers in perfectly square and in exact measurements. This has no structural disadvantage, but will lead to difficulty should someone later want to insulate the floor between the joists with solid foam panels.

We take a day off now and then, for some trout-fishing or blueberrying, often combining the expeditions with Lou and Ruth. It is a good year for blueberries at Pine River, and we bring back several buckets full. Enough to more than withstand Lynne's steady onslaught and still provide for pies and blueberry pancakes to help celebrate Sally's birthday. I lead a botanical field trip to Jackman Pond, complete with canoes, and Lynne presides over her hundred or so Cecropia caterpillars which she has raised from eggs. Big and juicy from a summer of ravenous eating of black cherry leaves, they are dressed in glaucous blue-green accented with blue, red, and yellow knobs. They are beginning to spin their cocoons, which Lynne will sell to Dr. McCann at the Dart-

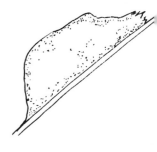

mouth Medical School, for her cardiac research.

Looking ahead to later roofing, we realize we'll need more rafters, so these logs are cut to about 4-6'' butt diameter and appropriate length, from smaller trees. Many of us take turns at peeling these. Even 83-year-old grandma Emlen peels one as her contribution. Then they are left in the sun to dry.

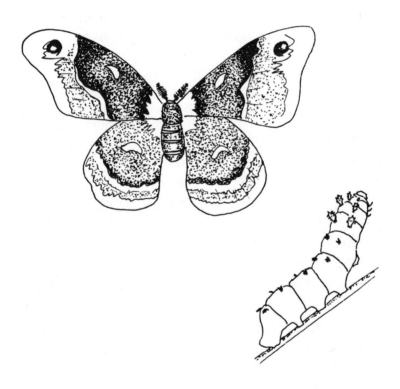

FLOOR SUPPORT

End View

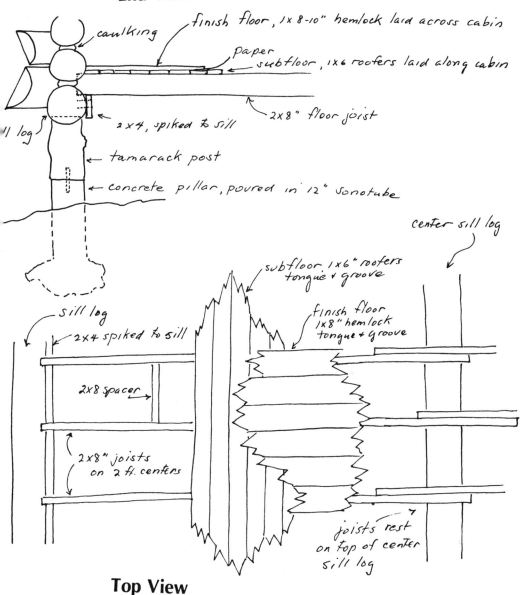

caulking

finish floor, 1x 8-10" hemlock laid across cabin

paper

subfloor, 1x6 roofers laid along cabin

2x8" floor joist

2x4, spiked to sill

sill log

tamarack post

concrete pillar, poured in 12" sonotube

center sill log

subfloor, 1x6" roofers tongue + groove

finish floor 1x8" hemlock tongue + groove

sill log

2x4 spiked to sill

2x8 spacer

2x8" joists on 2 ft. centers

joists rest on top of center sill log

Top View

Raising
the Cabin

Now the rush is on. We want to get the cabin up and the roof on before the snow should fly, a scant two months away. There are in fact only a couple of weeks before Chris and I have to return to our respective colleges. So we work full out, picking the logs, rolling them up the ramps, dogging them, marking, dogging and notching, placing, drilling and spiking.

The logs are laid butt-to-top all the way around; first two side logs, then two cross logs, then two sides logs again, etc. The saddle notch is easy. A cross log is rolled onto the two side logs

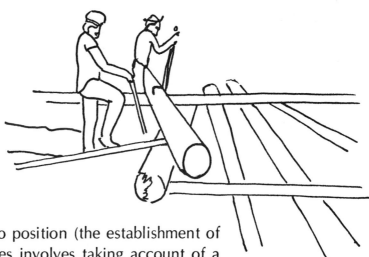

and dogged into position (the establishment of which sometimes involves taking account of a slight curve in the log which we like to face outward). The dogs are 2-foot-long steel bars (they could be longer) with 4″ right angle ends at each end sharpened to points; one end of the dog is driven into the cross log, the other into the side log, thus holding the former firmly in place. The cross log is then marked using carpenters dividers with a pencil in one side. The dividers are set to

either ½ the diameter of the log to be notched or else to the width of the opening between the log and the next parallel one below it. The latter procedure leaves you with practically no crack at all, but over several courses you can get to a situation where much more or less than half the log must be notched, and that is not desirable. The marks from each side join to make a saddle shaped pencil mark. After marking, the log is rolled over and dogged and the notches cut. We make a number of cuts with the chainsaw down to the pencil mark; then the notch is quickly chipped out with an axe. Both notches of a log can usually be cut in less than ten minutes, allowing for a fitting or two. The log is then rolled into position, and the space between it and the log beneath it will range from none at all up to a half inch or so. Most of the notches show a tight fit, but there are a few that don't. These have been cut by one or another volunteer more novice than expert with the axe. Perfection has to be compromised a little here, because some of the helpers should have the fun of doing more interesting jobs, learning in the process. We spike each log to the one below at each end, using 12 inch lengths of ⅜ inch reinforcing rod, having first drilled through the upper log with a brace and bit. This is a process I will later realize is absolutely unnecessary. When I do the thinking I should have done earlier, it becomes obvious that the alternating saddle-notches at the corners hold the logs rigidly in position, and no spike is necessary. But the spiking we do at each side of future door and window locations is important — it keeps the logs in place after the doors and windows are sawed out, before the frames are nailed in.

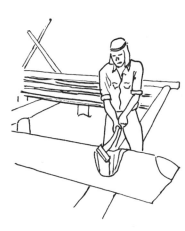

Chris, grown big and very strong in his 19 years, is the tireless driller of most logs.

Some of the August days are hot and still, and sweat pours off our glistening backs and trickles into the stomach creases above the belt line, mingling with sawdust and flecks of bark. That is

when the clear cool water of the pond beckons us a mite early, and we hurry down the path to jump into its cool embrace. The dogs always accompany us excitedly, but never swim. From centuries of selection Sheltie genes obviously run

CUTTING THE SADDLE NOTCH

each step done at each end of log; log is dogged for all steps
(dog not shown in steps 1-4)

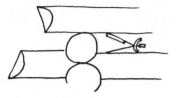

1. set dividers

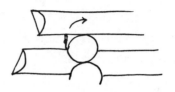

2. hold dividers perpendicular
and begin to scribe

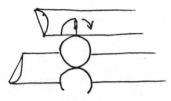

3. continue scribing up
and around

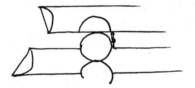

4. complete scribe and continue
on other side

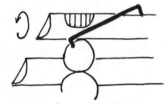

5. roll log over, dog, and cut
to pencil mark with saw

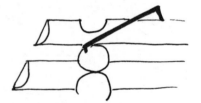

6. chip out with axe

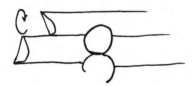

7. remove dog and roll into position

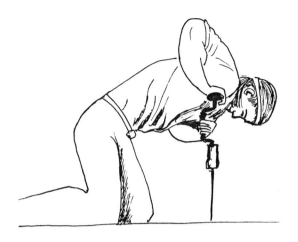

more toward herding sheep than chasing water-fowl!

Five new extra long logs for the purlins and ridge pole, to allow for the porch extension, have been cut and peeled and are drying on skids in the corner of the field, under the watchful eyes of Mts. Whiteface, Passaconaway, Paugus, and Chocorua just to the North. That high corner of the field, just out of the woods from where the cabin is taking shape, provides a breathtaking view of this Sandwich Range, the southern front range of the White Mountains. I rather hope I have the blessing of the spirits of the Pequaket and Pennacook chiefs, Passaconaway, Paugus, and Chocorua, for whom three of the four peaks are named.

Finally it is a time of asters and goldenrods. Though the bane of taxonomists, they are splen-

did in their blue and gold. Blueberries and rasp-
berries, following the wild strawberries of early
summer, have come and gone, and even the
blackberries are past. The swallows have gone.
There are crystal clear quiet days when warblers
in their quiet early-Quaker migration garb chase
each other in unquakerly fashion down the long

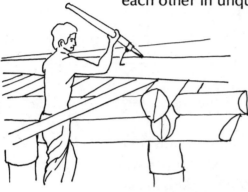

line of sugar maples and yellow birch at the edge
of the field. They are mute now, but playful and
excited nevertheless, perhaps in anticipation of
the long flight south, the yearly, star-oriented
voyage to new or dimly remembered lands far
away. Or maybe, in their breathless chases they
are practicing for next spring's sexual delights.
Occasionally the Pileated, that great king of the
woodpecker clan, will swoop out from the
deeper woods, calling with ringing authority. Shy
though he is, he has that quality of presence. It is a
time of harvest moon and the first frosts that will
kill back the tomatoes and beans and squash

(cabbages and collards, broccoli and kale — good cabbages all — will fight on for another month). Apples and pears and a few defiant grapes, challenging the northern latitude, are ripening. After dark but by the light of the moon the barred owls have two- and sometimes three-way conversations down in the valley of the Mill Brook. Maybe they're discussing plans for the impending trip south — I don't understand the words, but I love the resonant and decisive tones of their voices.

By our departure Labor Day the log courses have climbed to window-top level, when we saw out the windows with the chainsaw, then door-top level and the doors are sawed out. Before sawing, the extent of each opening is carefully measured and odd 2x4's or 2x6's are spiked temporarily in the vertical position — determined by plumb-bob — to establish the lines to cut to. In a bit of haste which I will regret, I let one of the sawed-out door logs drop on my foot, which gives me a probably cracked and very sore toe.

Then the long plate logs, which extend out over the porch-to-be, are placed. Some of these upper logs I roll up by myself, since Chris is gone. With some daring, a peavy, and wedge blocks I roll them slowly up the ramps to their position some 10 feet above ground.

From now on it will be weekend work excursions from Bennington, often with small groups

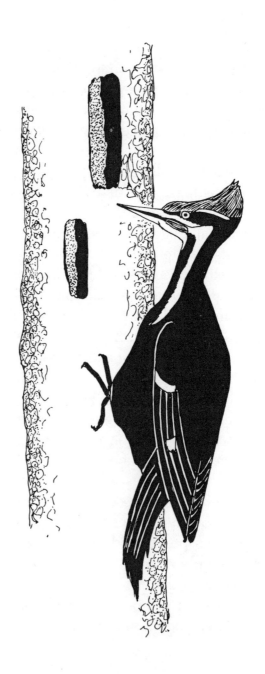

of students coming to help. Some are science
students, some are studying music or art or literature. There are folk-singers with guitars and
players of the recorder, mushroom buffs,
botanists, architecture students, and so on. Big
robust stews presided over by Sally, cheap red
wine and beer, sharp, pale New York cheddar cut
from wheels in the general store, and lots of
frozen vegetables raised in the big home garden
in Bennington all help power the working bodies.
The pond is cold now even as the autumn fire
reddens the maples on the slopes of the Sandwich
Range, but some of us are crazy enough to jump
in anyway. And smart enough to get out fast!
Lynne, bless her heart, is often more drawn by the
call of the wild than by the prospect of cabin
work, and she not infrequently goes on private
and meaningful expeditions across the road and
down to the beaver dams on Mill Brook. Above
and below the dams the lovely speckled trout are
spawning, their shy courtship over the clean sand

and gravel adorned now and then by the flash of the brilliant red bellies of the males.

We put in the four tie beams. I doubt that this kind of cabin needs that strength (tie beams hold the walls of a building from being spread apart by the weight of the roof), but it adds to the sense of strength anyway, and two of them will earn their keep by carrying the loft at the porch end.

Now we build up the gables with logs. The supply of dried logs has dwindled so that we begin to worry and conserve, piecing some, and running logs only to the loft window instead of all the way across. Piecing requires some sacrifice in looks, so if you have plenty of logs, it's better to avoid it. Each gable log is spiked at each end to the one below, but even so the gables, until fixed by the purlins, are floppy and need some braces inside and out. We cut some long red maple poles from the edge of the woods and prop the gables from the outside and inside both.

Placing the purlins turns out to be one of the

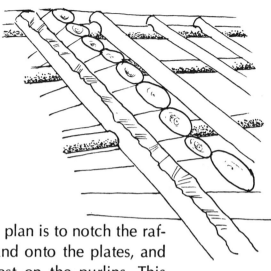

trickier maneuvers. The plan is to notch the rafters around the ridge and onto the plates, and
have the rafters just rest on the purlins. This
means the purlins must be exactly placed. We
goof a little here, getting the first set of purlins in
one course too late, but no matter, the only problem will be a slight matter of appearance, but no
one will notice. One of the purlins on the north
pitch has something of a bow and is set a little
high, and that will require us to use the fatter
rafters on that side, and notch them around that
purlin.

Alex and Charles help set in the top purlins and
then the ridgepole. These are big logs, 38 feet
long and straight. And heavy. We roll them up the
ramps and then horse them, an end at a time, into
position.

The leaves are off the hardwoods now, and it's
cold enough for gloves. When the ridge is in, we

55

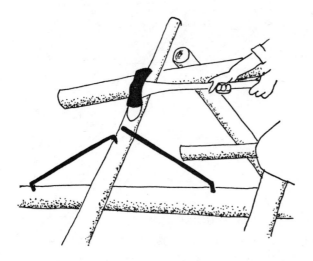

sit up there boastfully, some twenty feet off the ground, and insert a little fir tree into the spike hole at one end. That is an old tradition. But we don't have any champagne.

The gable logs are notched top and bottom around the purlins, so that the latter are not weakened.

By now we're into November and faced with the first snow squalls that bluster in from the West. We saw off the gables at the correct angle with the chainsaw, and we begin setting rafters at the east (kitchen) end. This involves high wire acts, the marking and notching being done from perches high on the purlins. I idly wonder if the Algonquin Pequakets had any of the qualities that have led to the more recent New York City Iroquois' reputed special talents for high construction. Each rafter is spiked to ridge, purlins, and plate with 8 in. galvanized boat spikes. These are army (navy?) surplus, contributed by Jim at the College; they are about ½ in. square in cross-section, chisel pointed, 8 in. long and have octagonal heads. Being galvanized, they are practically impossible to pull out, so after one mistake I learn not to make any more.

Some weekends are really cold, with spitting wet snow whipped by westerly gusts. Martha, botanist-to-be, shivers through one weekend with a blue and running nose. And my own nose has begun its usual winter behavior, with a constant poose on the end which never quite freezes. Albert's flashing red hair ought to lend more warmth to the scene than it does. His father is a contractor and Albert is handy with tools, and he helps put in the last rafters out over the porch. By now a good deal of the roof of the cabin proper has been covered by roofers, much of it capably and with great Italian humor nailed in place by Don and his son Mike.

As we get up close to the ridge with the roofers, the snow comes on strong, storm after storm, and we begin the process of shoveling off snow in between roofing operations. The diamond sparkle of the fresh snow in the sun eases somewhat the pain of the extra work. The pile of

ROOF AND GABLE

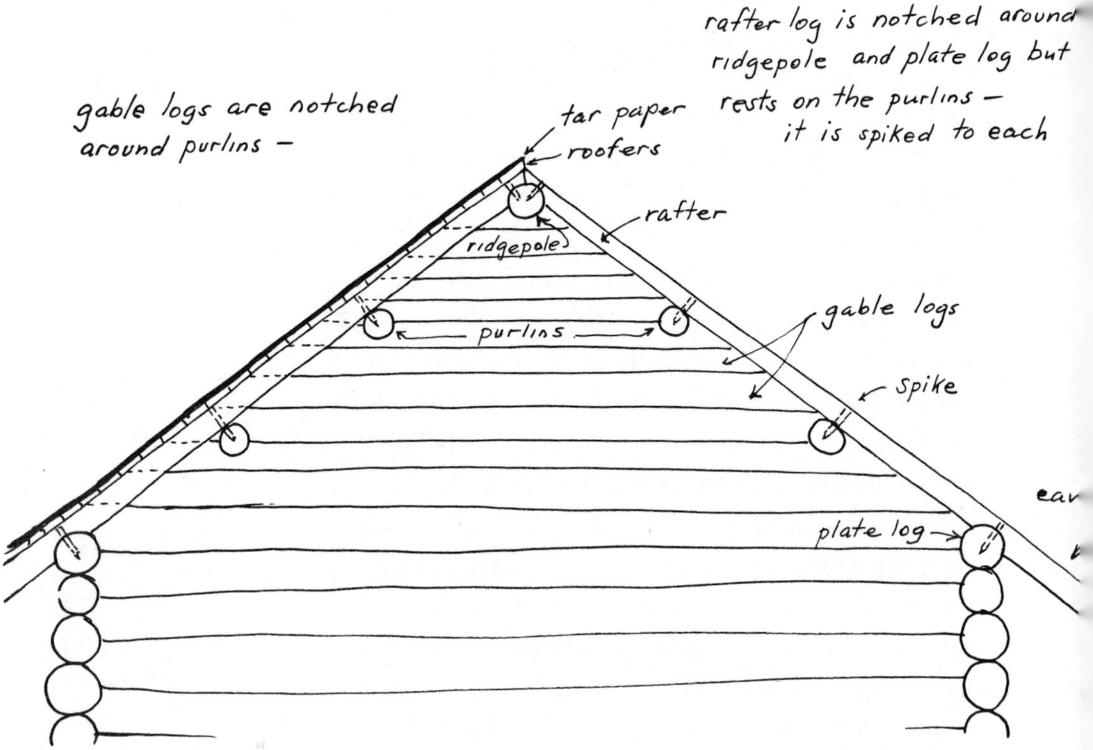

rafter log is notched around
ridgepole and plate log but
rests on the purlins —
it is spiked to each

gable logs are notched
around purlins —

tar paper
roofers

rafter

ridgepole

purlins

gable logs

spike

ear

plate log

Exploded Detail

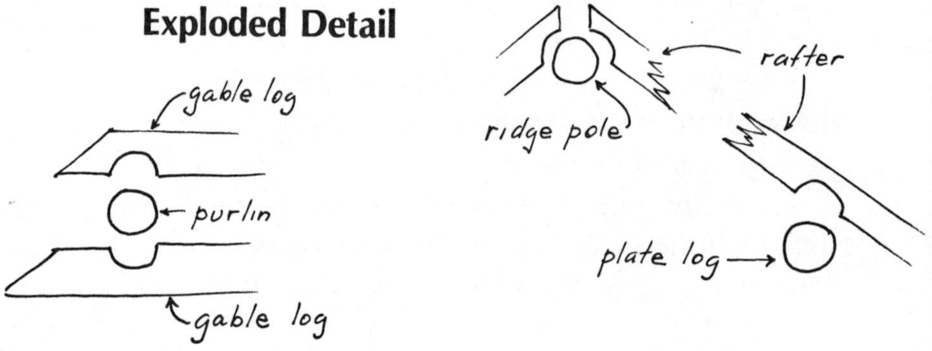

gable log

purlin

gable log

ridge pole

rafter

plate log

roofers on the ground is soon covered by a foot or more of snow, and when shoveled out, the tongues and grooves have to be laboriously cleaned of ice and snow, which we do with the claws of our hammers.

One weekend early in December Melissa and Lynne go off on a trek on snowshoes. There are fresh tracks in the snow, of fox and snowshoe hares, squirrels and mice, and even a bobcat. They finally discover a family of flying squirrels — a great thrill for Lynne, who with the help of a homemade "tree-bonker" has been searching for the better part of a year. At least two of the shy little creatures pop out of a hole in a sugar maple stub right in the woods back of the cabin, and one of them sails down the long and quiet glide to the base of a nearby tree.

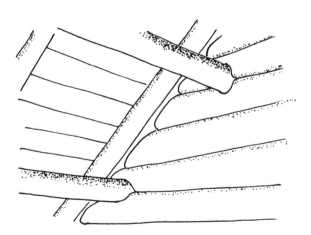

Thirty years ago Sally and I had a pet flying squirrel whom we dubbed, for reasons which have long since escaped me, "pigeon head." Some High Mowing students had been cleaning out bird boxes and came to one in the hole of which was a delicate little foot. They "corked" the box and brought it to me. Thinking it was probably a deer mouse, Sally and I uncorked the box and went to bed. Not long in the dark we were startled by a swoosh and a clatter, and lights revealed a beautiful flying squirrel upside down on a window curtain, looking intently at us with his huge liquid eyes. The lovely soft gray-brown coat joined in a crisp line along his side flaps with the clean white underparts. From then on pigeon-head lived with us, at first in a cage, then often loose in the apartment, gratefully munching on the filberts and almonds we gave him. He slept during the day in the bottom drawer of my bureau amongst the socks. The only two things wrong with that arrangement were first that I gained some fleas and second that one day when I thoughtlessly shut the drawer, he tried to chew his way into his bedroom, making a hole in the upper drawer face of Mrs. Emmet's nice old pine bureau. That took some explaining. Enough in fact to convince us that it was time for pigeon head to go free. And so he did.

There's something about keeping pets that speaks to and reassures the child in each of us. Like children, too, they can be wonderful receivers of love and kindness (both can be defenseless receivers of cruelty too but that is another matter). Also at High Mowing the students and I had a pet meadow mouse (vole) over in the Biology Lab.; it had been captured in the field by one of us. I don't remember what or whether we even named him, but we had great admiration for him. I have never encountered such a lion heart in such a small body. Absolutely fearless – or was it desperation born of fear? – he would at first stand up on his hind legs and threaten us with gnashing teeth – all two inches of him. But after he got to know us he became very friendly and loved to be lowered gently into the aquarium for his daily swim. He was an expert swimmer.

By Christmas we are roofed with boards but the snow, early as it is this year, lies a foot and a half deep on the ground, and there are great ridges under the overhanging roof, the accumulation from several successive shovelings. Chris is East from college, and during Christmas vacation we cover the roof with asphalt felt paper. Skye oversees the hauling of the rolls on a toboggan up to the site, a job that requires snowshoes for us.  The felt is a temporary measure made necessary by the fact that at this time of year I can not find any smooth-faced tar roofing rolls to buy, neither in Conway nor Bennington. Winter is not a time when people roof houses — and for good reason, among which are the difficulty of tarring joints in cold weather, and of handling the tar paper itself, which gets stiff and brittle. The asphalt felt paper is waterproof, though light and easily torn. We figure it will last till spring and keep out the wet, particularly if we fasten it down liberally with lath.

As if to add his two cents to our roofing concerns, Mucho gets up on the roof down at the house and then meows pitifully to be helped down. An old cat trick. Great cat that he is, his two faults are this delight in getting roof-stuck, and his initial terror of having to ride in a car. Whenever we drive to or from Tamworth, he sets up a painful, almost human yowling during the

first five minutes of riding. And as if to demonstrate definitively that psychosomatic or not, the distress is physical, he retreats back to the catbox and lets fly with something that instantaneously and completely fills the air of the car with what has got to be one of the worst smells on the face of this earth. Having made his point, he then settles down to sleep and is fine the rest of the way.

I'm pleased to see, with all the snow now looming in four-foot-high ridges under the eaves, that the sill logs are high and dry on their pillars. They are high enough, and the 2½ foot roof overhang helps shed the snow far enough out.

So the shell is up from its foundations and roofed in three weeks of daily work plus two and a half months of occasional weekends. Sheet plastic over the window and door openings

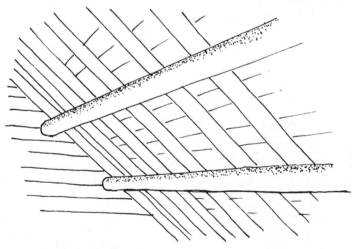

makes the cabin somewhat weather-proof, keeping out both snow and wind, so that work can go on inside.

In our rush to get roofed, I haven't noticed the gathering snow on the tool tent. Until too late. The tent gives up its ghost with a big tear from the weight of the snow. I regret I didn't take it down, but it was very old, a little holey and it served two generations of family well.

VIEW OF ROOF FROM INSIDE

*showing ridgepole, purlins,
rafters and roofers*

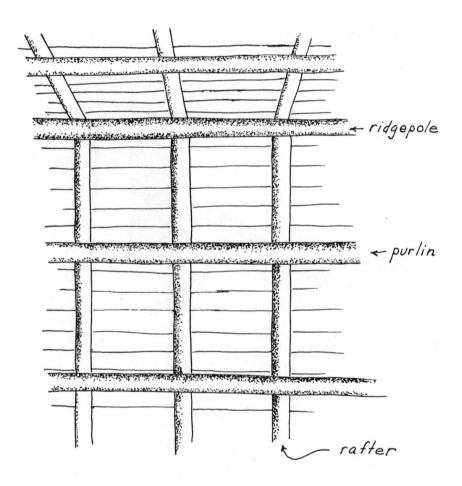

← *ridgepole*

← *purlin*

← *rafter*

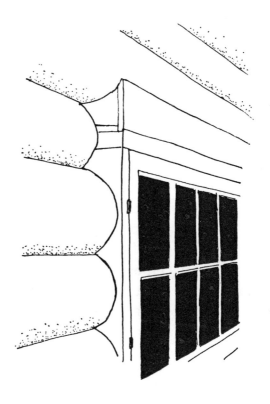

Finishing Off

Putting the subfloor in is next, and I run the roofers lengthwise across the joists. I leave a strip along each side sill temporarily unfloored, to allow air circulation for quicker drying of the sill logs, still damp from the spring rains.

A somewhat fussy job involves cutting and fitting small log plugs to go into the gaps between rafters at the plate logs along the sides. I worked out a way to cut the ends of these almost two foot logs with a chainsaw, each cut curved in such a way that the piece fits snugly into the space. The logs are then held in position by being nailed in through the roof.

And I begin door and window framing.

By early next summer I've cut and peeled some more logs to make 10 joists each 8 feet long and 3-5 inches in diameter, and Chris and I later in the summer mortise the ends of these, on 2 foot centers, into the two tie beams at the porch end. We run roofers across the cabin on top of these joists, producing an 8x16 foot sleeping loft. And I finish framing the doors and windows. The sides and tops of these are 2x8 inch spruce, the sills are 2x12 inches of, as it happens, western hemlock. The sills are put in sloping outward for drainage. All the pieces, earlier cut to proper length to just accommodate the 2x3 foot sash, are assembled and spiked together, then installed as a unit and spiked into the logs on the sides of the openings and bottoms. There is a 2 inch gap over each window frame and up to 4 inches above each door — these gaps are to allow for shrinkage of the logs. Although such was the recommendation of the books, in retrospect I hardly think such a

LOFT SUPPORT

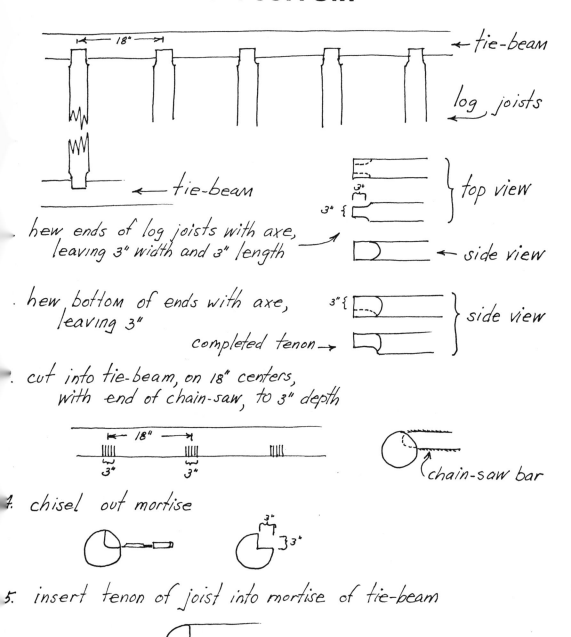

← tie-beam

log joists

← tie-beam

} top view

3" {

. hew ends of log joists with axe, leaving 3" width and 3" length

← side view

. hew bottom of ends with axe, leaving 3"

3" {

} side view

completed tenon →

. cut into tie-beam, on 18" centers, with end of chain-saw, to 3" depth

18"

3"   3"

chain-saw bar

4. chisel out mortise

3"   3"

5. insert tenon of joist into mortise of tie-beam

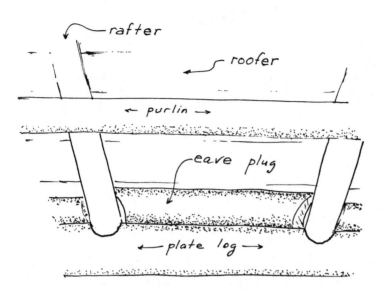

large gap is necessary.

Chris and I put the final roof on, running 65 pound smooth-face roll roofing from eave up over the ridge to eave, lapping and tarring the joints. A 3-in-8 pitch roof is a little too steep to stand on and work, so we have to use a wood ladder with cleats nailed on at the top at the correct angle to hold over the ridge, and also 2x4 inch cleats temporarily nailed in at various places in the as-yet unroofed part, to support either us or the bucket of tar. It is a relief to have the tarpaper on, for the felt had curled and shrunk in places, resulting in leaks when it rained. The final roofing is put on right over the felt, and now the cabin is absolutely rain-tight.

August arrives again. It is just a year ago that the foundations were poured. I have tongue and groove eastern hemlock for the finish floor. The boards look good and straight, but they were very wet when delivered, and in spite of having spent the summer stacked with spacers inside the cabin, are *still* wet. In desperation I lean them up against the eaves outside the cabin in the sun, and that helps some. First George and then Don work on laying the floor, which goes over paper laid on the subfloor, the hemlock running across the cabin at right angles to the red pine subfloor. It is nailed in with coated nails. In spite of being laid tight, the hemlock boards will shrink some more, later opening up some cracks. We apply clear floor sealer in two coats.

Finishing the windows falls to me: installation of ½inch pine stops against which the sash will

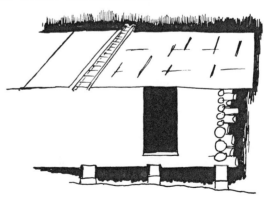

WINDOW

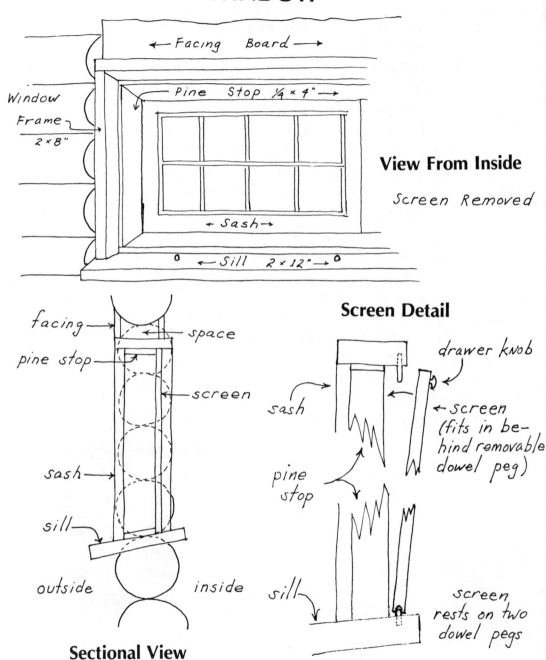

Facing Board

Pine Stop ¼ × 4"

Window Frame 2 × 8"

Sash

Sill 2 × 12"

View From Inside

Screen Removed

---

facing

space

pine stop

screen

sash

sill

outside   inside

Sectional View

Screen Detail

sash

pine stop

sill

drawer knob

← screen (fits in behind removable dowel peg)

screen rests on two dowel pegs

close on the outside and screens will fit on the inside; hanging the sash (hinged at the side to open as casements); and — fussiest job of all — boxing in the gaps above the windows and doors. The finished frames, by the way, have been put in far enough out so that the sash can open out and back completely, to rest against and be fastened to the log walls in warmer weather. Boxing involves fitting 1x6 inch boards, custom-hewn at the top case, from log to frame inside and out, stuffing the space between with insulation, and piecing in the ends.

Also in August, caulking begins. For caulking I have located oakum from a firm in New Jersey: tarred, twisted jute supplied in 8-stranded rope of about 2 inches in diameter. Depending on size of the crack, one or more strands can easily be separated, then driven tight into the cracks from

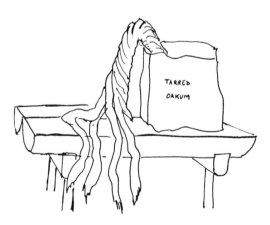

the inside with hammers and wooden wedges. The result is a good tight seal against weather. Caulking lasts into September, and a willing crew from Bennington College almost finishes it off: faithful Charles, plus Clay and Tom, and Lynne C.. Lynne C. unwittingly leaves her signature for posterity in the floor: some black scuffs and streaks from her boots as she hitches along banging in the oakum.

I hang the doors, which I've made from 2x6 inch tongue and groove spruce decking, with 1x4 inch hemlock cleats screwed to the inside. They are heavy, so large and rugged brass butt hinges are called for.

On a Saturday afternoon the crew mysteriously disappears while I am boxing windows, only to turn up at supper time with a basket of mushrooms. They have followed the mushroom enthusiasm of the Andres brothers· and returned with *Lactarius, Cantherellus, Tricholomopsis* and *Pluteus,* and a batch of the puffball *Lycoperdon umbrinum.* We all double check the books and try some of them with supper. The *Lactarius* is the peppery species — too hot for me. The puffballs we cook the next morning to garnish the scrambled eggs, and they are fairly good though somewhat gelatinous. Nobody gets sick.

One weekend is marked by a clear and beautiful impromptu recorder concert by Charles and Melissa, outdoors on the picnic rock, under the mountains in the gathering dusk. Another by guitar-accompanied folksongs by Cindy K. while we sit and gaze into the fire. Her voice is shy — almost hesitant — but very sweet.

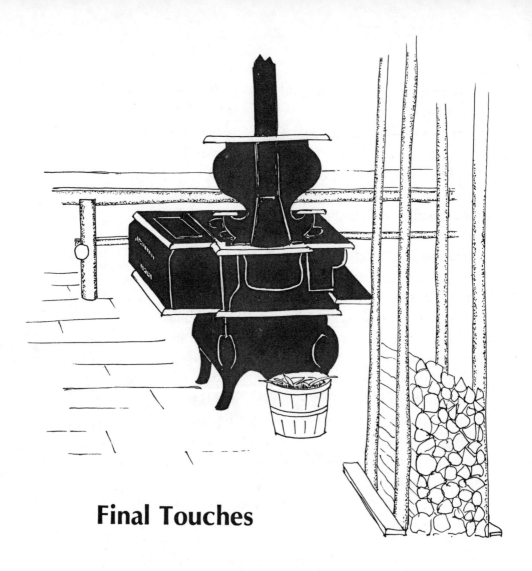

Final Touches

Through the second fall and winter there are a series of special inside jobs. I locate a second-hand farm wood range for $100. It is a large Glenwood model 540 with its water reservoir and side grates missing but otherwise in very good usable shape. I have a fellow in Claremont build a new reservoir, and a Bennington student of metal sculpture cuts some steel plates to line the fire-box. I've stored it in the barn down by my brother's house, and now we lug it in in pieces, reassemble it, and move it into position at the east end of the cabin, far enough out from where the counter will be, and just to the north of center. I run 6 inch stovepipe directly up, going through the roof with a section of metalbestos insulated pipe, held tight by the adjustable-angle brace piece the company sells. I've had problems getting the proper thimble for my roof pitch; after several episodes of the wrong thing being sent, I finally get a thimble. Though still not the proper one, it is close enough so I decide to put it in anyway, all the while according the wholesale supplier the colored adjectives appropriate to idiocy he so richly deserves.

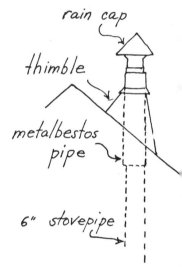

rain cap

thimble

metalbestos pipe

6" stovepipe

Occasionally when building a cabin, you get to thinking you know just about everything, and an episode like that of the thimble convinces you that the world is populated by people showing varying degrees of mental deficiency. But before you become insufferable, you make a mistake of your own, restoring some humility and balance. I can think of several charming personal examples of the genre. Like the mistake I make at least once a year of measuring an inside dimension with a

metal tape and forgetting to add the 2 inches for the width of the tape case. Or the time I was cutting some plywood with a skill saw on a table on the porch down at the house; the table is an old and battered one of maple with the drop-leaves up, and I wonder why the saw is going too slow, to find that I'm cutting through the dropleaf. I perform this gaff in Chris' presence — what a way to impress a son! Or the time that I carefully and tightly screw a grab-bar into the wall of the toilet at the house, later discovering that I can't move the pocket door that closes off the tub room from the toilet area.

Anyway, the stove is in and working, and it makes inside work the second winter very comfortable. There is plenty of dry split red maple from the original site-clearing, and I put in a crib of vertical poles from floor to tie beam to hold a good supply of wood right handy to the stove.

Next is a counter the full length across the east end of the cabin, with small peeled red pine poles for vertical and horizonal supports, and left-over hemlock flooring boards for counter top and shelving. Above the counter and to the right I build extra shelves for future food staples, and smack in the middle of the counter, under the large double east window, I cut in a stainless steel sink. There will be no running water — the sink will be supplied from a bucket of hauled water —

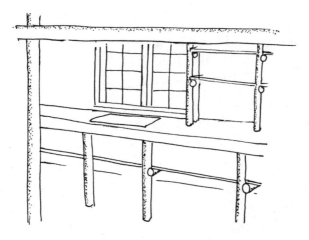

but I do put in a drain, including a plastic trap and pipe down out through the floor and into a French drain ten feet from the cabin.

It is now that I discover, in turning over an extra few spruce 2x6 planks piled at the edge of the loft, a swarm of happy carpenter ants busily house-making. They have already galleried one of the planks extensively. I regretfully take stern measures — a can of professional strength Raid. Having toiled and sweated so long to raise a cabin, I'm not about to see it chewed to pieces by ants. They prove to be as determined and persistent as they are reputed to be industrious, and it will be more than a year before I rout the last of them from along the porch end of the south sill.

In a way I envy the skill and vigor of the pileated woodpecker, who not only can locate the presence of carpenter ants deep inside large trees (how? by ant-produced air holes and sawdust? by acute hearing?) but also can dig them out with his great chisel bill, making the huge rectangular holes that are his trademark. It is interesting that both ants and pileated seem to like easily worked white pine. Just like skilled carpenters.

But envy notwithstanding, woodpeckers are not the way to go with ant control in a log cabin.

Chris and I build a log ladder, the rungs mortised and pegged into the side rails, that provides access to the loft. And I build two log couches at the porch end, under the loft. One of these is mortised and pegged into the wall logs, with plywood sections removable for easy access to stored stuff under. There are shelves at the head end of this one, for books, lamp, etc. The other log couch is movable.

The cabin is getting more and more comfortable, and during the second winter mice pay me the compliment of their presence. I never see them, since they are both shy and nocturnal, but their scats are about (what my father, in good German fashion, used to call Mäusedreck. By some sort of unspoken agreement, they leave the old horsehair double-bed mattresses in the loft alone — maybe they don't like horsehair, or maybe they're saving it till later, for dessert. They are almost certainly deer mice, *Peromyscus maniculatus,* which come into buildings in cold

LOG COUCH

Top Perspective

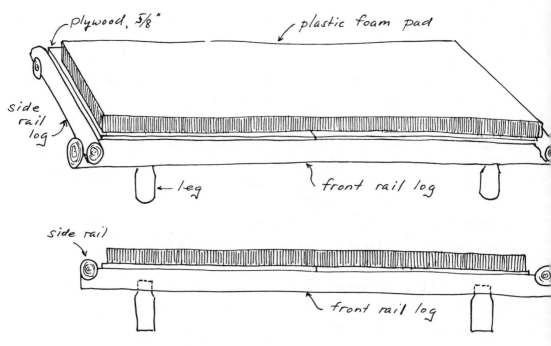

plywood, 5/8"

plastic foam pad

side rail log

leg

front rail log

side rail

front rail log

Side Elevation

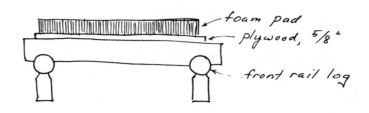

foam pad

plywood, 5/8"

front rail log

End Elevation

weather. From other encounters I know what lovely little animals they are, with soft, reddish-brown fur above and clean white below, and beady eyes that always seem to shine with excitement. I want to welcome them but know that later when there are more blankets and clothes they will chew them for nest material. And that will call for Draconian measures involving Mucho the cat or even De-Con.

The following (third) summer we finish off the porch. Nephews Art and David, plus Jenny,

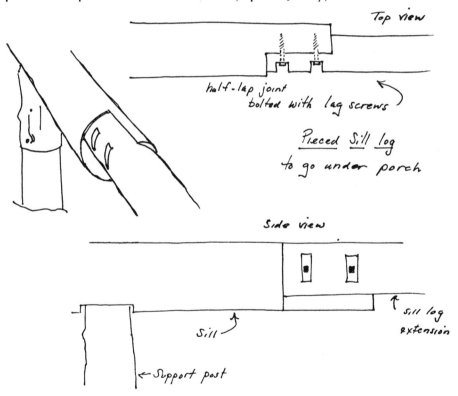

Top view

half-lap joint
bolted with lag screws

<u>Pieced Sill log</u>
to go under porch

Side view

Sill

Sill log
extension

←Support post

Lynne and I do this. Two of the three sills need to be pieced to extend out far enough, and we do this with half-lap joints, bolting the added log sections tightly to the sills. Then log joists, four of them, are run cross-wise, either resting on the sills or notched into them just the right depth to bring the porch floor to the right level below the porch door. 2x6 inch spruce planking is then nailed at right angles, with nail-head-wide spaces between for drainage. We set a chalkline at the outer edge to cut to; this is an interesting problem since there is no perfect line or reference point to measure from. So we eyeball it, set our end nails, and snap the chalk line. Jenny practices her crosscut sawing technique by cutting to it with a good sharp handsaw. Now I put in center and side vertical porch posts to support the roof and porch tie-beam, after which the temporary props that have served till now can be removed, and the porch is finished.

I build the screens out of 1x2 inch pine and aluminum screening, the simple 45 degree corners held with corrugated fasteners and L straps screwed in on the inside. The screens are planned to fit snugly against the stops from the inside. They have to remain easily removable so that the brass rod window closers can be operated from the inside. I decide on short dowel pegs on which holes in the screen bottoms fit, and a simple

TABLE (Collapsible)

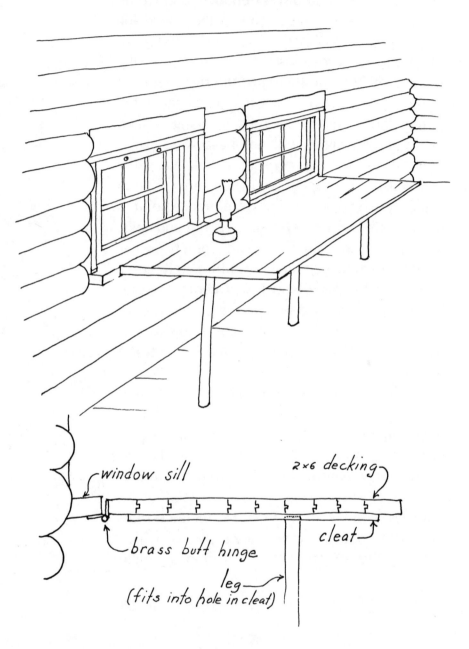

window sill

2×6 decking

brass butt hinge

cleat

leg
(fits into hole in cleat)

dowel peg inserted in a hole at the top middle. And two hand knobs on the top rail.

The table is put in last. It is 8 feet long and 2 feet wide, of spruce tongue and groove decking, 2x4 cleats screwed to the underside, and hinged to the window sills on the South side. Three removable round legs support it at level height. This way the table can easily be dropped out of the way to lie against the wall.

All this summer I have spent half time in Bennington, working with students in the Hopkins Forest in Williamstown. They are in a National Science Foundation Undergraduate Research Program, doing field ecological research. One of them, Kathy, is working on red oak reproduction; she stays in our Bennington house and looks after the large vegetable garden, keeping the weeds back and freezing the produce. She keeps things in good shape, and on each trip north I take loads of fresh vegetables to Tamworth (I've since started a smaller vegetable garden up there; we're now a two garden family). Lou also has a fine big garden, down beyond the barn, and he and Ruth generously supply whatever extra we need.

The Privy

The third fall is the time of the privy.

Privy building may be well on its way to becoming a lost art. Some thirty years ago I gained experience in it; part of my 3½ year service as a conscientious objector was spent in a hook-worm

88

control unit in Florida under the Public Health Service. The major work project of the unit was the building and installation of sanitary pit privies in the rural areas around Orlando (before Disneyland had been even dreamed of), as part of a campaign to reduce the spread of hookworm. There were about five of us working on this, and my recollection is that we got so we could produce fast enough so that we could build and install one a day. This was accomplished by modest mass-production methods at our privy plant, where we made the prefabricated sections: sides, back, front, roof, cribbing of pecky cypress, cement floor, cement riser, and seat of southern pine. The installation crew of two would then take the partially assembled privy out to the designated location, dig the 4x4x4½ foot pit, install the cribbing and then the privy. These were, I'm proud to say fine, sanitary, fly-proof examples of the art.

Even previous to that, when I was a boy I'd used privies. At that time we'd had a summer camp up hereabouts without running water, and hence a privy (which I remember was quite a haven for paper wasps), and at that time there were still quite a few in use in the countryside. Some of them were single holers, some two and even three holers. With liberal use of ashes, sand, and lime, they could be kept pretty much odor free.

More recently two working privies have im-

pressed me. One belonged to Dick and Barbara; a gray and weathered two holer with a door and curtained window facing south with a sweeping view across the Havard Forest in Petersham. It was a fine place for contemplation. The other, an example of ingenuity in the face of a difficult site, was Brooks' privy at his cabin on the rocky North Shore of Lake Superior. This was a single holer perched on a rock crag where the volcanic ledges drop precipitously to the gravel shingle of the beach, and surrounded by black spruce and cordifolia paper birch – a cold northern woods festooned with old man's beard lichen. Brooks had skirted the impossibility of digging a pit in the rocks by constructing a 10 foot cribbing down from the perched privy to the lower level. The result was dramatic and beautiful.

Now I sketch out a two holer that will have a door and window in the south side. There are odds and ends of logs left and some roofers. With the help of a large crew one fall weekend, and a smaller group on another, we get it raised in a secluded spot in a fir thicket, open to the South for warmth. It has a timbered frame with vertical siding, a sloping shed roof covered with tar paper, a nice casement window of barn sash, and a door opening in. Architecture student Blair is consulting architect. Cindy C. is there, her hair

long and nose a little red from the cold, and Cindy K. as usual is a tiger for work (later C.C. will do her senior thesis on the behavior of California sea otters, and C. K. will do hers on small mammal populations on Martha's Vineyard). Tia helps split firewood, keeping her feet well back from the danger zone as she tentatively attacks with the axe — not Paul Bunyan form, but prudent.

The riser I put in high (so high, in fact, that it seems made for giants, and I'll want to make a foot bench later), with two seat holes carefully cut out and differing in shape and position to provide more versatility for differences in age and sex. Charles has done the bulk of the digging of the pit; not only is he very bright, but also a tireless and capable worker. Sally S. builds the cribbing of old lumber scrounged from piles near

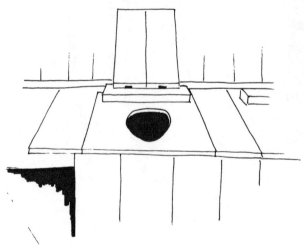

the ceramics studio at College, and it is lined with aluminum press sheets from the press room of the *Bennington Banner*. Cindy K. and Jyl do this while Michele and I are roofing, and contrary to expectation they put the printed side facing in. What this means is that anyone falling into the pit will be able to amuse him- or herself by reading the *Banner* — if he has matches or flashlight — while waiting for help. The *Banner* incidentally is a fine paper, and our use of their press sheets for this purpose in no way casts aspersions on it; instead it testifies to a bargain I couldn't resist: a bundle of the sheets for a couple of bucks.

New Wanderings

A year or two go by – they seem to do that ever more quickly now. The student friends who helped so much graduate or leave and go on. Sally sells Jessie and Peebles and starts to draw and paint again. Jennie hikes 900 miles of the Appalachian Trail with friend Steve; she gains in strength and wisdom, quietly investigating new

Ontario, still with clean streets and seemingly clean air.

I muse on whether Canada, big and young and still ingenuous, will be able somehow to save its beauties – it has so many left still. So in a way do the States, but in a half-century I have seen so much lost to inexorable and compulsive development. Will we learn to measure progress with a yardstick divided in units of quality? Can we reap the undeniable benefits of modern technology without destroying the soil out of which they spring? These are some of the questions being asked increasingly around the world, in Scandinavia, The British Isles, and Western Europe, in Japan, in Africa and South America, in Russia and India and China, and in the U. S. and Canada. There are enormous problems of employment, economy, human rights and provision for peaceful social change, of countries grown too big to govern and cities decaying in their centers, of societies like wastrels using resources as if there were no tomorrow.

There is a tomorrow.

Guarding it for ourselves and our children and their children, will require changes. We'll need, for instance, to get rid of such childish notions as the idea that we can grow endlessly in numbers and technology in a finite world. Or that peace somehow will miraculously come down from

Heaven to peoples frantically and mindlessly preparing for a war that is clearly unthinkable. Or that learning how to do something is somehow more important than being clear on what it is we're trying to do.

But these are big problems, and this is a small book about a cabin.

Finis —
More or Less

As I sit and write this in the cabin, the quiet showers of an August three-day northeaster are falling gently on the roof. Outside the myriad smells of woods in the rain rise with the mist, presided over mostly by balsam fir, which my aging nostrils can still enjoy. A fire in the stove has banished the chill and dampness, and the Coleman lamp hisses comfortingly. I can hear the raised voice of the little unnamed brook in the woods to the South, swollen by the rain. It is a brush-burning day and there is much to do, but I am nursing a tennis elbow, so opt for writing.

There are a few more things to do in the cabin, even though it is basically finished and certainly usable. The couch pads of plastic foam are covered now with orange cloth sewn by Carol, but I want to build a bench on the porch, for that is a lovely place to sit in the afternoon sun. And I've been cutting firewood from some of the thinned red maples around the site. Some of this I've had drying on the porch for a couple of months; that should be dry enough to burn later this winter. The front door steps are built and handles are fitted to the doors, latches still to come.

It's quiet here. I'm pleased with the cabin, and grateful to all those who did so much to help: family, students, friends. I think my mother and father, who bought the place about 40 years ago and loved this country, would approve. The spirits of all are about. When I get time, I'd like to carve the names, into a tie beam pehaps, of all those who helped. That's a lot of carving.

It will be possible for some to live simply here, from time to time, in close tune with nature, undisturbed and undisturbing.

And that is good.

100

APPENDIX

Some Log Cabin Books

Below are annotated a few of the many books on log cabin building. Many if not most of the older cabin books are out of print and hard to get. A few of them are excellent. In the last few years several new books have appeared which should prove very useful. The ones listed below are limited to those which I have seen. Since I did not do a complete "review of the literature," the absence of any book from the brief list below casts no aspersions on it. Other titles are annotated else-where (e.g. in Leitch, 1976). A complete survey of cabin building books is being prepared by cabin-builder John J. Viktora, P.O. Box 1165, Flagstaff, Arizona.

Aldrich, C.D. 1928. *The real log cabin.* MacMillan and Co., 278 pp. An older book, dedicated to Abraham Lincoln and illustrated with photos and a few line drawings.

Angier, B., 1952. *How to build your home in the woods.* Hart Publishing Co., New York. 310 pp. Angier loves the outdoors and his enthusiasm shows through on every page. The emphasis is on low cost, practicality, simplicity. Coverage is complete. There are lots of line illustrations — not the greatest artistically, but very informative. I found this to be one of the most helpful I used. Indexed. A good buy, it should still be available.

Bruyers, C. and R. Inwood. 1975. *In harmony with nature; creative country construction.* Drake Publishers, New York. This is a big-format book with lots of illustrations, both photos and drawings which are well done and informative. The book is imaginative, creative, yeasty, somewhat disorganized. It has no index. Should be very helpful.

Dillon, R.P. 1938. *Sunset cabin plan book.* Lake Publishing Co. San Francisco. 63 pp. Mostly floor plans for a variety of vacation cabins. The section on building a log cabin is too brief to be much help. No index.

Hard, R. 1977. *Build your own low cost log home.* Garden Way Publishing Co. Charlotte, Vt. 200 pp. This book has a great deal of information for the money, most of it reliably accurate (treatment of a few topics like wood decay organisms and vegetation maps leaves a bit to be desired). Approach generally practical and straightforward. A good part of the book concerns log-kit home construction. Illustrated with many line drawings that are not exciting but are informative, and some photos of reasonably good quality. More than usual coverage of, for example, energy-conserving siting and insulation. Extra information on stoves, manufacturers of log-kits, nail sizes, etc. in appendix. Indexed. Should be very helpful.

Leitch, W.C. 1976. *Hand-hewn; the art of building your own cabin.* Cronicle Books. San Francisco. 122 pp. The author deals with more than just cabins; he has written a book which includes a lot of intelligent and thoughtful comments on life-style, life in the mountains, self-reliance, versatility, etc. It is an encouraging, confidence-building book. The many photos, only a few of which are murky, show a great variety of approaches — cabins that have been built for the most part in the Northern Rockies. There is a good chapter on cabin books, a brief glossary, and an index. A fine book, and reasonably priced.

Mackie, B.A., 1977. *Building with logs.* B.A. Mackie and I.M. Mackie, Prince George, 76 pp. Large format, so you get more than you might think for the $10; still, a high price for spiral bound. Illustrated with drawings, which are excellent, and photos, which are acceptable. Mackie runs a log-building school and is clearly very experienced and knowledgeable. He tends to be, on some points, opinionated and dogmatic. There is, for example, a tirade against "cabins" and their builders — a discordant note in a book which includes many sound and intelligent ideas and lots of useful information. No index.

103

Mason, B.S. and F.H. Keck. 1947. *Cabins, cottages, and summer homes.* A.S. Barnes and Co. New York. Rather straightforward. Has some good line drawings. Includes chapters on adobe construction, frame construction, stone construction; only about a third of the book covers log construction. Lots of plans, including floor plans.

Popular Science Editorial Staff. 1934. *How to build cabins, lodges, and bungalows.* Popular Science Publishing Co. New York. 251 pp. A large part of this book deals with other types of cabins, refinements, modern conveniences. The part on log cabins, though not very complete, is well done, well illustrated, and informative. Indexed.

Rutstrom, C. 1961. *The wilderness cabin.* MacMillan and Co. New York. 169 pp. First chapters discuss different kinds of cabins and are illustrated with photos (rather dark). There are later chapters on tools, the building process, etc. There is only one brief chapter on building the log cabin; it is therefore only a very brief treatment of procedures. What drawings there are (not very many) are good. Some of the full page ink drawings, by Les Kouba, are very nice. No index.

Swanson, W. 1948. *Log cabins.* MacMillan and Co. New York. Small format, compact. Has floor plans of lots of cabins, line drawing illustrations. Very brief treatment of each item, but has information on extras like driving a well, dugout canoes, and dams. Indexed.

Weslager, C.A. 1969. *The log cabin in America.* Rutgers University Press. Not a how-to book, this is the social history of log cabins, from their introduction into North America by the Finnish and Swedish colonists (and into the West by the Russians via Alaska) through the famous "log cabin campaign" of 1840, which elected William Henry Harrison to the Presidency. Photos of historical cabins like that of Teddy Roosevelt in South Dakota. Fascinating!

Wiggenton, E. (ed.), 1972. *The foxfire book.* Anchor Books, 384 pp. The Foxfire Books are all worth having. This one has a section covering log cabin building which is well done. Deals appropriately with styles of the southern Appalachians using hardwoods, including details of various dove-tail joints. An excellent buy. Indexed.

Northeastern Tree Species for Logs

White pine *(Pinus strobus)* From Maine to Quetico-Superior, this tree can grow to towering giant size. Light, soft but strong, clean-cutting and easy to work, its wood is choice for furniture and building. The tree is an aristocrat that in colonial days was saved for masts for the King's Royal Navy. It is my first choice for cabins.

Red pine *(Pinus resinosa)* Ranges with the white pine, but not so widespread, found more often on coarser sandy soils and rocks. Often planted in plantations. It is also called Norway pine (for Norway, Maine, rather than for the Scandinavian country directly). It is a little coarser and heavier than white pine, and doesn't cut so clean. Still good.

Jack pine *(Pinus banksiana)* Smaller and often scrubbier than its white and red relatives, it can grow tall and thin on suitable sites that run to either coarse sands or the rocks of the Canadian Shield on the one hand, or to wet peat soils with black spruce on the other. Harder and coarser than white. But in pure stands it is nicely limb-less and scarcely tapers. O.K.

Red spruce *(Picea rubens)* The major spruce of mountainous New England and Eastern Canada, it grows tall and straight in even-aged stands. The source of spruce gum. Harder and heavier than the pines, it cuts very cleanly and is strong. A fine choice.

White spruce *(Picea glauca)* This is the spruce westward in Ontario and in the Lake States. It doesn't grow quite so even-aged and straight as the red, but it also cuts clean. Tends to be a little "knobby" at limb attachments. But O.K.

Black spruce *(Picea mariana)* This spruce is a typical bog species, though it also occurs as a prostrate shrub at timberline in the Presidentials. In Ontario and the Lake States, on less acid but still organic soils, it can grow tall and thin in pure stands or mixed with jack pine. O.K.

Northern white cedar *(Thuja occidentalis)* Usually occurs on moist sites; it can grow to fair size; boles may have a bend at the bottom. But it makes light, soft, fragrant, and decay-resistant logs for a cabin. A prime choice.

Tamarack *(Larix laricina)* Also called larch, this is another bog species which can also grow on moist uplands. It is the only northern conifer that is deciduous (the only other deciduous conifer in the East is the bald cypress of the southern states). Tamarack can grow tall and straight; its logs are rather hard and heavy. Good.

Balsam fir *(Abies balsames)* This is something of a weed species in the North Woods, though some is cut for pulp and it does make the very best Christmas trees — wonderfully fragrant. In the days before foam pads, campers used to make fir-bough beds. The wood is soft, coarse, and somewhat prone to decay, but if nothing else is available it could make a serviceable cabin. The liquid pitch blisters in the bark can make it messy to handle. Passable.

106

Hemlock *(Tsuga canadensis)* You could build a cabin from hemlock, but at younger ages it's apt to be a little limby. Also, the wood is harder and heavier than many softwoods. Its strength, so useful in barn and bridge timbers, isn't needed in log cabins. Its branches and knots can be hard enough to dull an axe in the cold of winter. Passable.

Popple *(Populus tremuloides)* Also called trembling aspen. A deciduous species and not a conifer, this is a soft "hardwood," a successional species in the Boreal and Lake States Forests (possibly climax on some sites in the Rockies). It can grow in extensive even-aged stands of straight-trunked trees. I don't believe I've ever seen a popple cabin, but I think it would be O.K.. The wood is soft, white, easily axed. Passable.

Western Tree Species for Logs

There are many more species of conifers that grow in Western North America, and most of them if even-aged and forest grown are suitable as sources of cabin logs (exceptions are the scrubby, open-grown piñon pines and junipers of the Southwest, which have multiple and crooked stems, and the timberline species which are stunted).

A few of the commoner are listed below.

Lodgepole pine *(Pinus contorta)* In the Rockies at higher elevations these trees grow tall, thin and free from limbs in even-aged stands. It is a fire-successional species. Logs are ideal for cabins and are being widely used for pre-cut log cabin kits. One of the very best.

Ponderosa pine *(Pinus ponderosa)* One of the most important and widespread timber species in the U.S., found at lower montane elevations through most of the Rockies, Cascades and Sierras, as a climax species. The trees grow to very large size. Trees in younger close-grown stands are fine for logs; can be somewhat limby in open stands. Wood cuts and works well.

Western white pine *(Pinus monticola)* Similar in many respects to Eastern White Pine. Occurs in Northern Rockies, Cascades, and Coast Ranges, but commonest on mountain slopes in Eastern Washington, Montana, and Idaho. Prime.

Engelmann spruce *(Picea engelmannii)* An important timber species of the Subalpine zone in the Rockies and Cascades. The trees grow tall and straight; wood similar to that of the Eastern spruces. Fine logs.

Colorado spruce *(Picea pungens)* Grows on mountain slopes of the Southern Rockies. In appropriate stands trees grow tall and straight. Can be limby, but useful for logs. Also called blue spruce.

Sitka spruce *(Picea sitchensis)* An important timber tree of the Pacific Conifer Forest. Found near the coast, from Northern California north into Alaska. Grow to very big size, so immature trees would be necessary.

Black spruce *(Picea mariana)* and White spruce *(Picea glauca)* Have already been described in Northeastern Tree Species section. Both species range across Canada and up into Alaska.

Western larch *(Larix occidentalis)* Like Tamarack but with longer needles, this species grows at middle altitudes on moist mountain sides of western slopes of the northern Rockies and eastern slopes of the Cascades. It is an important timber tree, growing tall and straight with little taper. The wood is hard, compact, durable. A prime choice for logs.

Tamarack *(Larix laricina)* Has already been described in Northeastern tree species section. Ranges west across Canada and into Alaska.

Douglas fir *(Pseudotsuga menziesii)* In the upper montane zone of the Rockies doug fir (not a true fir) is a climax species; it plays a more successional role in the Pacific Conifer Forest. One of the most important timber species in the U.S. Wood strong, heavy, durable. Grows to very large size.

Subalpine fir *(Abies lasciocarpa)* A higher altitude species in the Rockies, often associated with Engelmann spruce. Wood very light, not very durable, but useful for logs. Also called alpine fir.

White fir *(Abies concolor)* Grows straight, without much taper, in the Southern Rockies and Sierras. Wood is light, soft, coarse-grained, not durable. OK.

Red fir *(Abies magnifica)* On middle elevation moist slopes of Sierras. Nice logs. Wood is the heaviest of any fir and comparatively durable, though soft and easily worked.

OTHER WESTERN FIRS: Grand fir *(Abies grandis)* and **Pacific Silver fir** *(Abies amabilis).*

Western hemlock *(Tsuga heterophylla)* Grows in northern Rockies and Westward into Pacific Conifer Forest. A good timber tree, it can get quite large.

Western redcedar *(Thuja plicata)* This is an important

timber tree; its wood is light, straight-grained, durable. Grows with doug fir and western hemlock in Northern Rockies and in Pacific Conifer Forest. Choice for logs.

California incensecedar *(Libocedrus decurrens)* Grows on the Western midslopes of the Cascades and Sierras. Light, soft aromatic wood. Fine logs.

Coast redwood *(Sequoia sempervirens)* Ranges along coast region of northern California, in the so-called fog belt. The trees are taller and thinner than giant redwoods *(Sequoia gigantea)*. The wood is soft, brittle, straight-grained, red, very durable. Younger trees make fine logs. But species is probably being overexploited.

Popple *(Populus tremuloides)* Not a conifer. Grows in glades and groves in the Rockies, Sierras etc. and ranges from the East westward across Canada into Alaska. See Northeastern Tree Species section.

Order of Operations

Design — Design cabin; make scale drawings.

Site and Logs — Clear site. Cut needed number of appropriate size logs, peel, and pile to dry.

Foundations — Pour concrete foundation piers (or make them with rocks or log cross-cuts).

Sills — Establish level of sill bottoms; cut and install posts. Notch for posts the two side sills and center sill; install sills. Notch in first two end cross logs.

Floor Support — Spike 2x4 inch ledgers (joist supports) to side sills. Put in 2x8 inch floor joists on 2 foot centers; notch side sills to receive joist ends; spike in joists. Nail in spacers between joists. Put in sub-floor of 1x6 inch roofers, running lengthwise (across joists).

Walls — Build up walls with saddle-notched logs, butt-to-top all around, so that top of log is above butt of log below it. Keep inner faces of logs plumb. Spike logs to logs below at either side of future door and window openings. When log below the log that will be the plate of the windows is laid, saw out windows; brace logs between openings in plumb position. Spike temporary 2-bys across ends of logs in window openings to hold them in place. Continue up with walls till log below log that will be plate of doors is reached, then saw out doors. Spike 2-bys as with windows to hold ends in place; brace intervening logs temporarily in plumb position. Continue up with walls to main plate logs; install these so that they extend out over porch at porch end of cabin. Put in tie-beam logs and bolt in to logs below. Lay temporary boards across tie logs to serve as working platforms at gable ends.

Gables and Roof Support — Build up gables with logs to level of first pair of purlins. Notch in first set of purlins; these also extend out over porch end. Gable logs extend out in odd lengths, but must extend at least beyond the plane of the roof. Continue up to level of second set of purlins and notch them in. Build up rest of gable to ridgepole and notch latter in. When both gables are complete, with the two sets of purlins and the ridgepole in position, install first, end pairs of rafter logs against the gables. Rafters are notched around the ridgepole and plate logs and rest on the purlins. Using chain saw, saw off ends of gable logs flush with rafter logs. Continue to install pairs of rafter logs on 2-foot centers, the length of the cabin and out over the porch; spike each rafter into

111

ridge, purlins, and plate logs. By continual eyeballing, keep tops of rafters in line and level with plane of future roof. Cut off ends of rafters to measured projected roof overhang.

Roof — Nail 1x6 inch tongue and groove roofers, running them lengthwise and across the rafters, starting at lower (eave) edge of roof and working up toward ridge (tongue up, groove down). Use galvanized or coated nails. If necessary, use lath shims between rafters and roofers to keep roof straight. Hew top lines of roofers so they meet flush along ridge line. Determine proper overhang at each end of cabin; measuring from inside of gable logs out, snap chalk lines from ridge to eaves and cut to lines with a handsaw. Install eave plugs to fill spaces above plate log and between rafters; nail through roof into eave plugs to hold them in place. Cover roof with smooth-face roll tar roofing; run it from eave over ridge to eave, tarring joints. (An alternative roof: shingle with cedar shingles)

Porch — Porch can now be completed with cross-log joists and 2x6 inch decking nailed over joists with nail-head-wide spaces for drainage. When decking is in, support posts for porch roof can be put in.

Doors and Windows — Windows and doors can now be framed and frames spiked in to window and door openings (if logs are not dry, this spiking should be done in such a way as to allow sliding between frames and log ends as logs shrink; consult one of suggested cabin books for details). Install pine stops. Install barn sash. Make doors of planks (e.g. spruce tongue and groove 2x6 inch decking) and hang.

Floor — Install finish floor (lay paper between subfloor and finish floor). Finish floor boards run at right angles to subfloor boards.

Finish Jobs (can be done in any order) — Caulk cracks between logs with oakum. Install stove, stove-pipe, roof thimble. Build loft, supported on joists notched into tie beams. Build kitchen counter and install sink. Build couches, table. Make door latches. Build front door steps.

Privy — Build and install privy.

Glossary

Adze — a long-handled trimming or hewing tool with a cross chisel blade. Used to be used for finishing off squared timbers.

Auxin — one of the naturally occuring growth hormones in plants; chemically, it is indole acetic acid.

Browns *(Salmo trutta)* — brown trout; introduced from Europe, especially Scotland and Germany, and stocked in many U.S. bodies of water. They are successfully naturalized throughout most of the northern U.S.

Canadian Shield — that part of Canada with ancient granitic bed-rock.

Cant hook — used for rolling logs. Has shorter handle than peavey, a blunt end with a side edge for gripping, and a hinged hook.

113

C.D. — stands for Companion Dog; a level of achievement in obedience training of dogs.

Chalk line — strong string, usually housed in a metal case into which powered chalk can be poured thus impregnating line with powdered chalk. The line can then be stretched tightly between two points and snapped against the surface between, making a straight line.

Cecropia *(Samia cecropia)* — one of the most beautiful moths in the U.S.

Clinometer — an instrument that measures degrees (or %) above or below level. Can be used as a level.

Cribbing — a wood frame that fits into the pit of a privy and keeps soil or sand from caving in.

Cutter's (Cutter) — a modern insect repellant. Active ingredients are: N,N-diethyl-meta-toluamide, dimethyl pthalate, etc.

Decon — a brand of rat and mouse poison.

Deer flies — smaller cousins of the horsefly. Also called copperheads (they have copper-colored or green eyes). They can inflict a painful bite.

Deer mice *(Peromyscus sp.)* — the soft brown field mice with white underparts and long tail; they usually come into houses in rural New England. Also called white-footed mice, they are capable of climbing trees.

French drain — a pit or trench dug in the soil that is filled with loose rock. It serves to receive roof, storm, or sink drainage and allow it to dissipate.

Gables — the ends of the cabin, above sidewall height, that taper upwards to a point at the ridge.

High bush cranberry *(Viburnum trilobum)* — not a cranberry at all, but a tall woody shrub with showy flower clusters and, later, bright red and very sour berries that make good jelly.

Hobble bush *(Viburnum alnifolium)* — a woody shrub. Common understory species in the Northern Hardwood-Conifer Forests of northeastern U.S.

Ichneumons — group of parasitic wasps of the order Hymenoptera, family Ichneumonidae.

Joists — the strong supporting cross-members to which the floor is nailed.

Ledger — 2x4 spiked lengthwise along inner face of sill log, upon which ends of floor joists rest.

Line level — a small (2″) bubble-in-liquid level that clips onto a (chalk) line.

Log dog — a two or three foot steel bar with short, right angle bends at each end which are sharpened to points. The sharpened points are driven into the logs, thus holding the loose one firmly in position for notching.

Meadow mouse *(Microtus pennsylvanicus)* — now more commonly called vole; small, common, gray-brown, with a short tail.

Mortise — a squared hole cut into a log or timber or board. Into this hole the tenon fits.

Muskeg — acid bog, usually of appreciable extent. May

result from filling in of glacial lake, or may be a "blanket bog" on flat terrain. Characterized by very acid conditions (due especially to Sphagnum moss), and shrubby vegetation especially of the blueberry family. Two tree species occur: tamarack and black spruce (both usually stunted).

Northeaster — in New England, a protracted summer storm with cool rain showers; frequently lasts three days. Winds are from the northeast.

No-see-ums — very small (barely visible with the naked eye) insect pest. Also called minges, punkies, etc.

Oakum — tarred, twisted jute. Used for caulking cracks between logs.

Off — a modern insect repellant. Active ingredient mostly N,N-diethyl-meta-toluamide.

Peavey — a strong pole fitted with a metal point and hinged hook, for rolling logs, prying, etc.

Picaroon — a long-handled pick-like tool with a sharp point for picking and moving logs.

Pine stop — ½x4 inch pine boards, nailed to inside of window and door frames so that windows, doors, screens, and screen doors fit in against them.

Plates — top logs of side walls; lower parts of rafters rest on them.

Plumb-bob — brass, top-shaped, and sharpened to a point, it is suspended on a string to indicate true vertical.

Privy — outdoor toilet without plumbing. Also called outhouse.

116

Pulp hook — a short, pointed, hooked tool for handling pulp logs; similar to a hay-bale hook.

Purlins — main, lengthwise supporting logs of roof between ridgepole and plates; the rafters rest on them.

Rafters — poles or two-bys that run from ridgepole, resting on purlins and plates, and extend as eave overhang.

Raid — insecticide sold usually in pressurized cans.

Ridgepole — top log running lengthwise from gable to gable; supports rafters at top.

Roofer —usually 1x6 inch tongue-and-groove; boards used in roofing, subflooring, etc.

Sable — Shetland Sheep Dog with brown (golden, rust; to dark) and white coats, the brown hairs usually tipped with dark.

Saddle notch — Some authors use this term for the kind of notch used in the cabin in this book (upper log notched halfway; lower log not notched at all). Others use the term "round notch" to a lock-notch joint that has both upper and lower logs with straight, "roof-pitch" notches that mesh. This has led to some confusion. I use the term saddle notch instead of round notch.

Sandy outwash — usually coarse-textured soil (sand) deposited by outwash from melting glaciers. Such coarse sand areas usually support jack pine, northern pin oak and red pine in North Central U.S., and pitch pine-oak stands in the Northeast.

Sash — the window proper with its glass fixed in position.

117

Shad *(Amelanchier sp.)* — any of several species of short to tall shrubs or low trees. Called shadbush (because showy white flowers bloom about the time the shad used to run up the New England rivers to spawn); or Juneberry (because berries, which are good for pies, ripen in June).

Sill (of door or window) — the bottom member of a door or window frame.

Sills — the two bottom side logs, the first one in each side wall. The sills rest on foundation pillars or posts and support the first cross logs or end walls.

612 — a modern insect repellant. Active ingredient is 2-ethyl-1,3,hexanediol (612-Plus has N,N-diethyl-meta-toluamide added).

Sonotube — hard cardboard cylinder used as forms for pouring concrete cylindrical posts.

Speckled trout *(Salvelinus fontinalis)* — the eastern brook trout. The native trout of eastern U.S. Also called brook trout, squaretail.

Spud bar — an iron bar flattened and sharpened to a chisel edge at one end. Used for peeling bark off logs; also, a long version used to be used for splitting off blocks of ice when ice was cut from ponds and lakes.

Steelhead *(Salmo gairdnerii)* — very large rainbow trout that run out of large bodies of water (ocean; large lakes) into streams in the spring to spawn.

Tenon — the squared end of a log, timber, or board cut to just the size to fit tightly into a mortise.

118

Tie beams — cross logs laid across a cabin from plate to plate; they are notched over and bolted to the plates. Generally tie beams hold walls fixed against the spreading force exerted by weight on the roof.

Tricolor — a Shetland Sheep Dog with black, white, and brown coloration.

Trilliums — any of several species of the genus *Trillium,* which are showy herbaceous spring wildflowers of the lily family.

Vascular cambium — the circumferential layer of cells in woody plants that by dividing produces new wood on the inside and bark on the outside.

Vascular rays — sheets of cells that have a radial orientation in woody stems, function in lateral transport inward and outward.

Voyageurs — the French Canadians who transported, by canoe, supplies westward and furs eastward in the early fur trade in northern U.S. and Canada. Renowned for feats of strength and endurance.

Index

120

122